2009 Poet

I have a dream 2009
Words to change the world

Martin Luther King

John Lennon

Lancashire
Edited by Donna Samworth

First published in Great Britain in 2009 by:

 Young**Writers**

Young Writers
Remus House
Coltsfoot Drive
Peterborough
PE2 9JX
Telephone: 01733 890066
Website: www.youngwriters.co.uk

Foreword

'I Have a Dream 2009' is a series of poetry collections written by 11 to 18-year-olds from schools and colleges across the UK and overseas. Pupils were invited to send us their poems using the theme 'I Have a Dream'. Selected entries range from dreams they've experienced to childhood fantasies of stardom and wealth, through inspirational poems of their dreams for a better future and of people who have influenced and inspired their lives.

The series is a snapshot of who and what inspires, influences and enthuses young adults of today. It shows an insight into their hopes, dreams and aspirations of the future and displays how their dreams are an escape from the pressures of today's modern life. Young Writers are proud to present this anthology, which is truly inspired and sure to be an inspiration to all who read it.

Contents

The Poems

Dreams

When we were told that night,
Your future seemed far out of sight,
We were told you had a clot,
But to me that didn't mean a lot,
We all had a weep,
And that night I cried myself to sleep.

They found something else, cancer they said,
At first this didn't stick in my head.

Today I went to see you,
Hannah and Mum came too,
You looked well,
But we didn't go to dwell,
All the family were there,
We didn't talk about your illness - we didn't dare.

Today I was told that the end is nigh,
I wanted to hug you and never have to say goodbye.

Today you were quite bad,
Hannah and Mum came back looking sad,
I couldn't bring myself to come,
Things were flying around my head,
So hard like a tricky sum.

On Sunday night you were terribly bad,
Hearing this made me really sad,
You kicked off at the hospital at 5am,
You screamed and shouted at them.

You didn't want to be in hospital and die,
But this we kind of knew why.

You got worse and they took you back in,
You knew with this illness you couldn't win,
You went unconscious and couldn't talk,
You couldn't open your eyes - but my gosh you fought.

Today they said it could be tonight,
Yes Dad, your future's out of sight.
It's been nearly four years since we last spoke,
I saw you in my dream, until I woke.

Rebecca Grinton (17)
Blackpool & The Fylde College

1

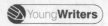

Beside The Beach

When I have my worries
And I've got no money
I go to a place which takes me away
Away from the problems I've encountered today
I take a walk, for it's a sunny day.

Dig my feet into the silk cut sand
And hear the rhythm from the pipe flute band
It's taking me away from reality
And as I watch the flight of the birds and bees
I am certain this is what it's like to be free.

As I strip off my clothes and dive into the sea
The water flushes all of the sorrow and joy
That is hidden deep inside of me
I feel reborn, I let time slip by
I'll float on this water till the end of time.

As I gaze at the stars and my body stays calm
The moon shines at me with a glorious charm
I get the feeling this is where I belong
Not in the slums of the government's arms.

And as I take one step off the beach
I step back into reality
I lose all meaning of what it is to be free
And it feels like my happiness was just a dream.

Happiness is something we find
Which we should make the most of from time to time
And even if it was a dream
I will float on the water till it's reality.

David Simpson
Blackpool & The Fylde College

Dream

I have a dream
Walking on the brink of a glass tile
Sparkle bridge glittered
Silence occurred
What did one more step mean?

Not just Earth but eight others
The corner of my eye dazed
One huge fireball looked upon my face
And brought off heat so sweet
Twinkle balls danced around my head.

Movement of time increased
Earth built up its rotation
My eyes gave a twirl and a roll
Colours separate and divided up
From primary colours to others.

The universe composes an image
One black room with colour and shape
Cylinders and blobs of those twinkle lights
One giant experiment
To know how it was formed.

My curiosity awaits
What is beyond those lines
Where Man has not been
I consider black carries out
Another cylinder to come.

Jordan Ismond
Blackpool & The Fylde College

Dream Dad

I have a dream,
I will go to work with my dad,
We will be happy together.

Subhan Younas (13)
Broadfield Specialist School

3

Driving Dreams

I had a dream,
I went to the car shop,
I got a Ford Focus,
I went to college,
To learn how to drive,
I got to the peaceful countryside,
And I felt happy.

Benjamin Littlewood (12)
Broadfield Specialist School

My Big World

Keep the world clean and tidy,
Don't throw rubbish on the floor,
Put it in the bin,
Don't bully people,
If someone is annoying you, tell a parent,
Put a sign up on the canal bank
Tell people not to throw rubbish on the floor.

Levi Green (13)
Broadfield Specialist School

The Cool Dream

I have a cool dream,
A nice world with lots of countries working together,
No fighting,
Stand up to hatred,
Never be bullied,
Everyone likes this world.

Jonathan Leach (12)
Broadfield Specialist School

Dream Rap

This is Blake Calverley, Bad Boy Blake,
And I have got a dream,
To make a better life for everyone,
Caring, sharing, no more bombs,
Everyone eating and drinking,
Not throwing litter, we want a better life!

Blake Calverley (14)
Broadfield Specialist School

Follow The Wind

I have a dream,
No more fighting,
Only love and respect,
Nature and our world,
Follow the wind!

Rachael Dixon (12)
Broadfield Specialist School

I Have A Dream

I have a dream that bullying never existed,
That hurting and hating never came to this world,
Tears turn to laughter and hate turns to real friendship,
I have a dream which will come true?

Simone Stratton (12)
Broadfield Specialist School

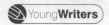

I Have A Dream

I have a dream
I hope that everyone respects each other
And works as a team,
To make our world a better place.

Sam Fennell (12)
Broadfield Specialist School

My Big World

Keep the world clean and tidy,
My world should save money,
Save water and electric,
Help the environment.

Timothy Kinsley (14)
Broadfield Specialist School

My World Dream

Hey, this is Nathan and this is my world dream,
This world should be peaceful and united.

Nathan Whalen (13)
Broadfield Specialist School

We Are Equal, No Matter What

I have a dream, day and night,
That we will accept black and white,
Respect each other's differences,
And not have any preferences.

A prison called Guantanamo Bay,
Where hate and death happens each day,
Torture is fuelled by racism,
Guards are poisoned by sadism.

But finally, the Red Cross came,
For no money, for no acclaim,
They cured each prisoner, let them stand,
Brought hope to this broken promised land.

A small child looks up to the sky,
From a sweatshop in Mumbai,
Working for nothing, he's poor and weak,
Is only paid one pound a week.

But he spoke out and was set free,
From this grieving monstrosity,
He now goes to school, he's content,
With his life, one hundred percent.

So although there's still hate on Earth,
There's a new chance with every birth,
Think about that, through your existence,
And accept, without resistance.

Gavin Neil (13)
Central Lancaster High School

It's Not Cool To Be A Bully

Every morning before school,
She fears, in case her clothes aren't cool,
She sighs, knowing how her day will be;
It's not cool to be a bully.

Scared, trembling, she looks around,
Hoping to be swallowed by the ground,
He sees her and knows she can't flee;
It's not cool to be a bully.

He walks over, she stands. Frozen still,
Like an animal going for the kill,
He hits her hard and painfully,
It's not cool to be a bully.

As she walks alone to class,
She pulls down her sleeve, to hide the gash,
Dearly hoping no one will see,
It's not cool to be a bully.

She's too terrified, too scared to tell,
About her life, this living hell,
Scared of what the consequences would be,
It's not cool to be a bully.

After thinking it all through,
She knew what she would have to do,
To tell was the only way she could see,
It's not cool to be a bully.

After she told, it stopped that same day,
And the school bully stayed away,
For once she felt happy!
It's not cool to be a bully.

If everyone would speak up,
The bullies would surely stop,
Bullies would no longer be,
It's not cool to be a bully.

Remember to speak out loud and clear,
So that everyone can hear,
So everyone in the world can see;
It's not cool to be a bully.

Molly Pye (13)
Central Lancaster High School

City's Powers

We walk along the streets alone
The people silent as a stone
Stealing our lives by the hours
We're trapped by the city's powers.

Street gangs take life and give back pain
In the cold and polluted rain
Building tops of concrete towers
We're trapped by the city's powers.

Think of the injustice of life
Fear and stress as sharp as a knife
We seem to think time is ours
We're trapped by the city's powers.

New generations infected
By their lives being reflected
Streets as grey as dying flowers
We're trapped by the city's powers.

But I can see a better place
No street gangs or crowds in your face
No more city's poisonous showers
No longer trapped by its powers.

Samuel Card-Hall (12)
Central Lancaster High School

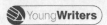

Don't Twist The Knife

I have a dream . . .

That those who are victims shan't suffer,
I hope that they will become tougher,
That they aren't suffering in silence,
And there's no more domestic violence.

They ask why as the first fist strikes,
There's nothing they're allowed to like,
Why is this such a problem in silence?
Why are they suffering in violence?

Why have a child if you just beat them?
When they really are your precious gem,
Why have the language of silence?
Why are they suffering in violence?

That one day all of this will stop,
Their confidence will not drop,
Into a brand new, better life with no silence,
Nothing to live in fear about, stop the violence.

I have a dream . . .

Danny Hodges (12)
Central Lancaster High School

An End To Bullying

I have got a personal dream;
A place where everybody's face beams,
A place where bullying people ends,
Why can't everybody be friends?

Some people bully to impress,
Or because of the way others dress,
Or because a happy friendship ends,
Why can't everybody be friends?

Bullying doesn't make you cool,
If you think it does, then you're a fool,
Be kind to people to start new trends,
Why can't everybody be friends?

Some people bully out of anger and hate,
But all the victim wants is a mate,
This is my wish, which all depends,
On everybody being friends.

Dale Pye (13)
Central Lancaster High School

I Don't Believe In War

I do not believe in any war,
It will make our country dim and poor,
People in fear of getting shot,
I have a dream that war will stop.

War causes a lot of pain and fear,
Because death is always near,
And the death count only goes up,
I have a dream that war will stop.

I do not like this violence,
I wish the stupid war could be silenced,
War is just to see who is on top,
I have a dream that war will stop.

I wonder if pacifists are right,
That we should end this pointless fight,
And all the weapons should be dropped,
I have a dream that war will stop.

James Schofield (13)
Central Lancaster High School

My Dream Is To Stop The War

War in countries is the issue,
Don't throw it away like a tissue,
Poverty's standing at the door,
My dream is to stop the war.

People fight to sort out this mess,
Trying to stop all this distress,
Greedy people, wanting more,
My dream is to stop the war.

Dead bodies lying on the street,
Seeing the coldness that they meet,
Countries that pulled the short straw,
My dream is to stop the war.

This long war is in Afghanistan,
All because of one evil man,
Very sick people wanting no more,
My dream is to stop the war.

Luke Gribbin (13)
Central Lancaster High School

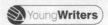

The Streets

Children sit sadly on the street,
Kicked out, starving, with nothing to eat,
They don't deserve to be left to roam,
Their dream is to find a home.

Sleeping in doorways and on the floor,
No pennies to their name, they need more,
Lonely and always on their own,
Their dream is to find a home.

The drunken, the beaten, the sad and the hopeless,
The lonely, the wailing and the young parentless,
Are all troubled, miserable and alone,
Their dream is to find a home.

Angry, sad, lonely and defeated,
Haven't even got a clean bed,
No friends to call on the phone,
Their dream is to find a home.

Rebecca Howarth (12)
Central Lancaster High School

Unexpected

I have a dream; will this war ever stop?
So tired, I think that I could drop,
Soldier's last fan with friends at the bar,
Before they fly off into the stars.
I don't want disruption among the ranks,
Go tell the commanders of the upcoming tanks,
Hopefully not tanks, planes and men of war,
This country now is just a huge bore.
I'm prepared for unexpected things to see,
Oh help me, I plea, someone help me,
I want peace to happen, a ceasefire,
This is my wish, my own desire,
We look with our eyes and then we see,
This is what you have done to a man like me.

Joshua Bate (13)
Central Lancaster High School

The Vote

In a line, they stand and wait like statues,
They're all so nervous as they stand, wishing,
The candidates, hoping that they will choose,
The crowd falls silent to the hushing,
As people gather, voting together,
Each other in union, today alone,
On one day a year, mankind forever,
People across the world watching at home.
The votes are counted, the results are in,
The silence hovers, the moment is set,
The polling is closed, they hope they will win,
The people at home, who have placed a bet,
The stadium echoes, the crowd shouts out,
The candidate is in, without a doubt.

Lewis Hamilton (13)
Central Lancaster High School

15

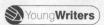
Manmade Disaster

Everyone has left the past behind
And they're riding in their fancy cars,
But the fumes are not being very kind,
Some say they will drive us all to Mars.
Global warming is one of the warnings,
To tell us to stop and look around,
The sky is grey in the early mornings,
Terrible discoveries have been found.
Think of the polar bear, on melting ice,
And all because we won't just stop and think,
It's not us who have to pay the price,
Our strange world could be over in a blink,
Extinction, climate change, poisonous gases,
We keep polluting as the time passes.

Rose Haigh (12)
Central Lancaster High School

Homelessness

I have a dream, right here this minute,
In which homelessness people are safe and sound,
They own just one outfit that fits,
Carers should be glad to have them around.
They shouldn't receive a dirty stare,
People should respect their situations,
We take our homes for granted, with no care,
Please give them your commiserations.
I have a dream, right here, this;
Where I think homelessness should be a crime,
The side of the street, they sit in a pit,
As they think, *will there be a home time?*
So this society should co-operate,
To help them put right their dirty state.

Sophie Ollerton (12)
Central Lancaster High School

One Kind Heart

Who is that old man, with a fear-stained face?
He's all alone, there's dirt across his feet,
His skinny-boned body, crumbling on the street,
He has dull, coal eyes which stare into space.
He's wearing dirty rags, not the Queen's lace,
He's starving hungry, wishing for some meat,
His stomach rumbles with every heartbeat,
He sees people thinking, *what a disgrace!*
They pass by leaving him in the corner,
But one kind heart smiles a conversation,
A few sweet words make his life much warmer,
She gives a pound with no hesitation,
She smiles, laughs and waves, then goes her own way,
One small act of kindness, made that man's day.

Elizabeth Reade (13)
Central Lancaster High School

A Dream To Deal With Discrimination

I have a dream to change the world forever,
There's no prejudice or discrimination,
We all accept and we work together,
No matter what your language or nation.
Uniqueness is believed to be a joy,
People are treated with equal respect,
No difference between a girl and a boy,
No more bullying and people learn to accept,
Height, race, accent, background or colour,
Disabilities, appearance or weight,
These differences don't really matter,
A world of love, laughter and no hate.
People aren't bullied because of differences,
We all realise we all have variances.

Danielle Powell (13)
Central Lancaster High School

From Dream To Reality

I have a dream, with some reality:
Racism will soon be intercepted,
Any race is allowed in our city;
A black woman gives birth to a white kid,
In our world there is no authority,
Black or white, you will not be neglected,
Black and white, together we will soon be,
All people are forever protected.
White or black, together we can be free,
Ban racism, you won't be rejected,
White or black, you are accepted by me,
And maybe white people are not hated.
I dream that black and white will soon be friends,
And all is OK when racism ends.

Loren Nott (12)
Central Lancaster High School

I Have A Dream

I start dreaming,
Wake up screaming,
I squeeze tight,
In a fright.

I want my dad,
I need him bad,
But he's gone,
I can't hold on.

I cry those tears,
All these years,
I turn back fast,
I can't bring back the past.

I always cry,
It's hard to say goodbye,
I can't breathe,
Why did you leave?

I love you so,
My heart will never let you go,
I lie in my bed,
And wish, I wish I were dead.

I need you,
I don't know what to do.

Danielle Clark (15)
Crosshill Special School

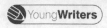

What If?

What if
The world was poor no more?

What if
The wars would just stop?

What if
Diseases never spread?

What if
The world could live in peace and harmony?

What if
Droughts never struck?

What if
Everybody shared the same love all around the world?

What if
Our dreams came true?

What if
We could help stop the wars?

What if
We could stop poverty?

What if
We could prevent disease spreading?

What if
We could stop droughts from endangering lives?

Dreams can come true as long as you believe,
Imagine the world like this, wouldn't it be a nice place to live?

Alex Tankard (12)
Holy Family College

Fight For Your Right

So you say that words can't change the world,
You can't stand up to bullies; racists
And you can't say what you feel.

Yet you feel so small and so quiet,
Scared of what people would think,
If you argued back.

You're black; they're white,
They refuse to even look at you, let alone talk to you,
You don't say a word, not even a slight mumble.

Words said intentionally about you,
Sniggers, as you walk past,
'Coward' they hiss or 'Chicken'.

You scamper where no one sees you,
Cry in the lonesome midst,
Of a dark, lugubrious room.

And it's worse when you go home,
There's no place to hide,
Neglect and hatred you feel.

Locked in a bitter, sinister room,
It's like they want you to die,
They give up, if you don't stand up for yourself.

However say a simple phrase,
Stand up for your rights and it'll go away,
It can all change.

Hiraa Jamil (12)
Holy Family College

21

Uncle Peter

My uncle Peter was my dad's brother,
His only brother and he loved him like no other.

Fifteen years ago, an illness took over his brain,
And it caused him great pain.

My dad was there to hold his hand,
To help him through and to make him understand.

He had many operations to give him extra time,
But we all thought he would pull through fine.

He was left with no sight,
Although he tried to make the rest of his life a delight.

My dad became his eyes when he took him out for rides,
Chatting and joking as they ate meat and potato pies.

His passion for Liverpool FC, he could no longer see,
Although he enjoyed listening to it on 'Radio 3'.

His bowls he could no longer play,
Because his sight had taken this pleasure away,
His bowls now belong to my dad,
And when he uses them he feels sad.

We have a picture of you, that stands at home,
We love you Uncle Peter,
You will never walk alone.

You left a place in my heart that no one else will fill,
I love you Uncle Pete and always will!

Beth Howarth (13)
Holy Family College

My Dog!

My dog
Brad is his name,
He is a Labrador,
He is brown and also a cutie,
My dog.

My dog,
He is the best,
He sleeps and eats,
He is a very lazy dog,
My dog.

My dog,
He loves to eat,
But also he loves to sleep,
My dog wakes me up for school,
My dog.

My dog,
He is so soft,
I love him so, so much,
My best pet in the whole wide world,
My dog.

My dog,
Love him very much,
Woof, woof, what does he mean?
I have had him from when I was six,
My dog.

Daniel Smith (13)
Holy Family College

What A Wonderful World We Live In

How magnificent to feel the warming sun,
Beaming down like an open fire,
The trees gently blowing in the soft breeze,
Looking like flexible bending wire.

The sea stretching out for many miles,
Like a twinkling sparkling lotion,
The graveyard in the dead of night,
With scarcely any motion.

The noise of snow underfoot,
With its crisp and crunchy sound,
How welcoming feels the rain,
When the sun melts the tar on the ground.

So beautiful is the springtime,
When the first flowers rear their heads,
And the birds are all in full 'song mode',
When we are just rising up from our beds.

The softness of a mother's touch,
When she first holds her baby near,
The overwhelming joy this special time brings,
So sweet . . . yet so salty the tears.

What a wonderful world we all live in,
If you just stop, look and listen for a while,
Maybe you will see then what I see . . .
It all makes me want to smile.

Tylah Tomkins-Simpson (12)
Holy Family College

Dreams

I have a dream,
That there is no violence.

I have a dream,
That there are no wars.

I have a dream,
That we can all live in peace.

I have a dream,
That we can all be friends.

I have a dream,
That nobody will be bullied.

I have a dream,
That nobody will be judged.

I have a dream,
That everyone is included.

I have a dream,
That everybody will live happy lives.

These dreams seem impossible,
These dreams won't come true!

But there is someone who can help,
That person is . . . *you!*

Louise Seale (11)
Holy Family College

My Cousin, James - Cinquains

My James,
He's my cousin,
He was great to play with,
We had so much fun together,
My James.

Later,
We had great fun,
Until he turned 18,
He went out then, left me alone,
Oh man.

Oh James
When I found out,
My dad said, 'James has gone,'
I burst into tears crying, 'Why?
Oh why?'

James, James,
I miss you so,
Even though you have gone,
I know you're still with me my friend,
Night-night.

Grace Roberts (12)
Holy Family College

Inspirational Dad!

The person who inspires me
And always makes me glad,
Who teaches me a lot of good,
And sometimes bits of bad.
Who always has a smiley face,
And never one that's sad,
Is my 24/7, all year round,
Inspirational dad!

Kristian Kershaw (11)
Holy Family College

My Inspirational Poem

There is a key in all of us,
It can bloom into a great talent,
But it is your decision if you want it to flourish,
Follow your dreams,
No matter what it takes,
The path to success is covered with bad temptations,
Don't let anyone get in your way,
When it gets tough, remember
You haven't failed until you have quit trying.
There comes a time when you must stand alone
But do not be afraid.
Stand up for what you believe is right,
And speak out for what you know is wrong.
Aim for perfection,
But don't be disappointed if you don't reach it,
No one is perfect at everything,
As long as you did the best you could possibly do,
There is a time when we have to leave,
So don't let any opportunity pass.
Follow your dreams . . .

Dominic Huckbody (12)
Holy Family College

Believe

Doctors believe they can save people's lives,
Environmentalists believe they can save the planet,
Footballers believe they can win.

Neil Armstrong believed he could reach the moon,
Kerry Anne believed she could reach the top.

I believe you can make a difference,
I believe you can do anything.

What do you believe?

Rachel Jackson (11)
Holy Family College

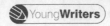

Think

Take a few seconds to just do one thing,
One thing only . . . *think*
Think what would happen if everyone was the same,
No one different
Think what would happen if there wasn't black and white,
Think what would happen if we betrayed our friends
To get to where we want to be,
Think what would happen if no one cared -
Not even our own flesh and blood,
Just because *you* were different,
Think what goes on in a victim's mind,
Think what goes on in a bully's mind,
Think, is there such a thing as Heaven?
Think, is there such a thing as Hell?
Think what would have happened if God didn't exist,
Think what would happen if the war never stopped,
So next time you are tempted,
Just do one thing and one thing only . . .
Just think.

Melissa Shannon Turton
Holy Family College

My Granny - Cinquain

Ma gran
She small and sweet
But with very small feet
She gives me money all the time
Ma gran.

Dear Gran
You gave me care
But now you are gone, where?
I think of you all the time now,
Dear Gran.

Jack Cairney (13)
Holy Family College

Caring For Life

They give up time
To help save lives
And really do it well.

That's why they care for life.

They train and train
For cuts and bleeds,
And even near death as well.

That's how they care for life.

They don't get paid
For all their work
That means they don't do it for themselves.

But still they care for life.

Most of these people are your age
And think it's really fun
And also help to save lives of people like you and me.

St Johns, that's how you can care for life.

Chloe Hobson (11)
Holy Family College

My Great Grandad

He's one hundred and three,
He hopes he could be me,
He doesn't need a stick,
And he can hold more than a brick,
He can climb up steps,
But he can't do any reps,
I love my grandad,
He's like another dad for me,
All he does is pray,
Each and every day.

Danial Tahir (12)
Holy Family College

29

My Cousin, Dawn

Cousin,
Dawn, you're a pain,
But in a good way, it's a
Good thing you make me laugh and smile,
Ha-ha.

You are
Weird Dawn, but
In a good way, you eat pickled
Onions, you eat them like mad,
That's weird.

You're always
Happy Dawn, but sometimes moody,
But what's the point when you're like that?

Watches drama series and more,
She's dramatic and funny,
There's nothing else I would like to say,
She's a great Dawn!

Emma Robinson (11)
Holy Family College

My Inspirational Poem

They always love me,
They always keep me warm,
They give me shelter in a beautiful home.

They always help me,
Even if I'm scared,
This is why they are always there.

They are always by my side,
They will always be my guide.

They cheer me up when I am sad,
This is why they are my mum and dad.

Daniel Titmass (12)
Holy Family College

Rio

He is fast, as fast as lightning,
He reads the game like we read a book,
He is strong, as strong as a bull,
His name is Rio Ferdinand.

He has passion, so proud of his country,
He has a heart, like the three lions on his badge,
He plays with full commitment,
His name is Rio Ferdinand.

When he tackles, he never loses,
When he jumps for a header he reaches the sky,
When he passes he always finds his target,
His name is Rio Ferdinand.

When I grow older I hope to play for England,
I will be the best defender anyone has ever seen,
Because my great inspiration,
Is a man called Rio Ferdinand.

Matthew Bagshaw (11)
Holy Family College

Friendship

Friendship is a lovely thing,
When you hear it, the bells start to ring.

Open the door,
Open your eyes, you will see the light of their guide.

Through the days,
They're by your side,
Your one and only true guide.

Shout out bad,
Shout out good,
They're always there,
When they should.

Chloe Hamer (12)
Holy Family College

31

Scary Guy!

If I could be anyone,
Who inspires me the most,
It would be the scary guy,
Who was the perfect host.

I met him at school, some time ago,
But the message he gave me will never go.

'Don't judge a book by its cover,'
Was the message he gave,
What an inspiration to all the lives he's changed.

Honesty and respect,
Loyalty and love,
How could I be without them?
They fit just like a glove.

I have learnt that it's not just about receiving
But to give on to others for my life to have meaning.

Joe Lundergan (13)
Holy Family College

Imagine . . .

Imagine a swimmer winning the gold,
Because they believe they can

Imagine a footballer scoring the perfect goal
Because he believes he can

Imagine a pen in a hand
That writes the perfect book
Because that author believes they can

Imagine you being someone else's inspiration
And they believe they can do what you did.

They believe that they can
And so can you.

Emma Foran-Leech (12)
Holy Family College

32

My Mum

My mum is wonderful,
Unlike a footballer,
My mum works for a living!

Ask yourself a question,
How much does Ryan Giggs get paid?
How much does a midwife get paid?
Who works harder?

A nurse, a policeman, a fireman,
They save lives every day,
He will get paid more in a week,
Than they get paid in a year.

Who would you rather have?
A footballer - who kicks a ball around,
Or the emergency services?
I know who I'd rather choose!

Bryony Sherry (12)
Holy Family College

I'm Inspired By . . .

I'm inspired by the world's tallest man,
I'm inspired by A C Milan,
I'm inspired by a very small can,
I'm inspired by everything.

I'm inspired by a cup of tea,
I'm inspired by an oak tree,
I'm inspired by a golden key,
I'm inspired by everything.

I'm inspired by the words,
Of a grown man,
In his own world.

I'm inspired by everything.

Teri O'Brien Corns (11)
Holy Family College

33

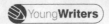
My Nana

My nana is the star brightening up my life,
Without her I would not know what to do,
She is always there,
Wherever I am.

> My nana is the best,
> And she is always looking after my dog,
> Called Bess.

My nana is like a doctor,
Whenever I am ill,
She looks after me
And she gives me a magical pill.

> I love my nana,
> She is kind,
> And nice,
> And she is my nana.

Thomas Marshall-Jones (12)
Holy Family College

Inspiration Poem

I love to dance,
I love to move,
I love to pop,
I love to groove.

When I dance I feel inspired,
As well as afterwards, very tired.

My all and everything goes into my moves,
With the pumping music and my new grooves.

I love to dance,
It's what I do,
I love to dance,
How about you?

Olivia Flanagan (12)
Holy Family College

Weird - Cinquains

This is
The night of one
The night is very dim
She howls away in the moonlight
It's her

Morning
She is awake
She walks down the hallway
She's awake, looks in the mirror,
Oh no.

That night,
The moon is low,
She pretends to be it,
This is the night that she has died.
Oh no.

Katie O'Connor (11)
Holy Family College

My Future

Listen,
Tick-tock, tick-tock,
I'm thinking, but what of?
What I will be, time passes me by,
Tick-tock.

Looking,
I see myself changing, growing older,
I look back, I see the old me,
Lost, help!

Trying,
To find something is to lose something else,
The me I lost has faded, gone,
I've changed.

Summer Goodall (11)
Holy Family College

Future - Cinquains

Future
Depends on you,
Recycling and litter,
Future will be all about you,
Future.

Future
The world could stop
And spin into darkness,
The green trees could bleed with lava.
Future.

Future
Whole new planets,
Aliens in my mind,
Before my eyes it all is changed,
Future.

Sarah Wolstenholme (12)
Holy Family College

What Is Your Dream?

Dream of birds walking and humans flying,
Dream of the oceans above you and the sky below,
Dream of growing money and raining seeds.

Dream of having holes instead of your nose,
Dream of moving pictures,
Dream of automatic cars.

Dream of shoes that can run as fast as cars,
Dream of gloves which grip onto anything,
Dream of robots doing all your work.

Dream of how you would feel if you never woke up
And kept on dreaming . . .

Joe Man (12)
Holy Family College

The Australian Bushes

Peaceful,
Australia,
Until this burning moment.
The bush fires were horrendous,
Troubled.

Troubled,
Trapped, tilted,
Make the world live in peace,
There are deaths all over, stop them,
Bang! Bang!

Bang! Bang!
The fire has spread,
Nothing can stop the heat,
Pray for those who have lost members,
Silence.

Jaymee Fletcher (12)
Holy Family College

There's Only One Chance At Life

There's only one chance at life you know,
With some emotions high and some emotions low.

Some things are clear, some things are not,
Some things are remembered, some things forgot.

Some things are up, some things are down,
Some people are serious, others are clowns.

Some things are good, some things are bad,
Some things are happy, some things are sad.

Everybody's different in a unique way,
And everybody's has a unique way.

Chris Whipp (12)
Holy Family College

Help! - Cinquains

Here now,
In the future,
All on my own like a . . .
Dead woman in an old coffin,
I'm scared!

Listen,
Nothing, nothing,
Absolutely nothing,
When you hear nothing, you are scared,
Have fear.

You died,
I didn't die,
I've got that special cure,
Now the future is at the end,
Help me!

Daniel Nixon (12)
Holy Family College

The Artist

I had a dream
That bears could dance
I had a dream
Sunlight could prance
I had a dream
Birds had painted wings
I had a dream
It rained a silver storm
I had a dream
Of the tiniest thorn
I had a dream about the person who dreamt all this.

Jessica Bogusz (12)
Holy Family College

In The Future! Cinquains

Peaceful . . .
Community,
No World Wars or fighting,
I want it to be full of peace,
Friendship!

Sunny,
And colourful,
Flowers are everywhere,
Animals welcome on the streets,
Kindness!

Fresh air,
No pollution,
Nothing bad in the air,
The sea is as clear as crystal,
Life's good!

Sophie Cheetham (12)
Holy Family College

Ambulances

They work in green,
The lights red and blue,
Saving people's lives, including me and you.

They're faster than a roadrunner,
The noise so loud, *ne-naw, ne-naw*,
All the cars move aside,
Saving people's lives, maybe me and you.

Jessica Adams (12)
Holy Family College

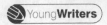

I Admire

I like,
This boy, so much,
He is, so sweet, so kind,
He is my knight, my dream, my life,
My heart.

One day,
I'd love to wish,
To be the right one,
For him, to be loved forever,
In love.

I want,
The right one now,
Now and until I die,
I would love to know if he loved
Me too.

Natalie Shackleton (11)
Holy Family College

Scream, Aim And Fire - Cinquains

Cover,
Scream, aim and fire!
Use the walk, make your way,
God had spoken through His conscience,
Now shoot!

Alpha!
I am English!
My name is Marcus Hawk,
My squad name is Alpha Zero,
Team out.

Go and
Defend yourself,
Run through the main barracks,
Meet the other group at crossfire,
Playtime.

Joshua Whelan (11)
Holy Family College

My Family

Hear this,
You're always there,
If I am miserable,
Or if it is a happy time,
Families.

Listen,
I hear laughter,
I hear lots of tears,
I hear my family having fun,
Families.

Thank you,
I love you all,
You've made my life so good,
I'm so grateful I have you,
Families.

Olivia Pring (11)
Holy Family College

Robinho - Cinquains

He has
The greatest feet,
He is great with the ball,
He is a midfield magician,
He's great!

He is
One of the best,
People can't tackle him,
Defenders fall down on their bum,
He's best.

When he
Is on the ball,
No one can tackle him,
When he's in the air, he is good,
The best.

Daniel Gibson (11)
Holy Family College

Life - Cinquains

People
Always smoking
At a very young age
Drinking a lot of alcohol
People.

Children
Playing around
They are very messy
Messing around with noisy toys
Children.

Life is
Being destroyed
Because people are bad
Time to take some action with this
Right now!

Nicole Adams (11)
Holy Family College

Believe

Believe you can do it,
Believe in yourself,
Believe in other people.

Believe.

Believe that it can happen,
Believe in anything,
Believe in everything.

Believe.

Believe you will get it if you try,
Believe nothing is impossible,
Believe anything is possible.

Believe.

Believe that you can achieve.

Katie Slinger (11)
Holy Family College

Admire

The person I admire,
Is Shaun Ellis,
He works with wolves,
And has given up a lot of his life for them.
He sees wolves for what they really are,
Not the evil, bloodthirsty beasts that people imagine.

He understands them better than anyone,
And is part of their pack,
His wife and four children left him,
Because he cares for the wolves the way he does.
But still he carries on,
Despite all this,
He is the wolf man,
And he inspires me.

Stephanie Middleton (11)
Holy Family College

I Dream . . .

I dream the darkness is broken,
Broken by a beam of light,
The light is focused to the stage,
The stage where I am stood.

The world where image is the main key,
Where everyone will dream to be me,
A career based on fashion,
One for which I've always had a passion.

My face on the magazine front,
Everyone will wish they pulled my stunt,
Airbrushed to perfection,
Everyone wants my complexion.

I reach the end, pose and turn,
Back to the dressing room I return.

Olivia Carter (14)
Kirkham Grammar School

I Have A Dream For Education

'Educated girls become educated women and those women
influence entire families, communities and nations'.
Source: Women and Global Human Rights, paper
Ravensbruck College, USA 2000 AD.

In China a father turns his head away from the first
Piercing scream of his beautiful newborn child.
Soon she will swallow the husks of paddy rice
To slit her delicate throat.

In Bangladesh the perfect dark-skinned child
Is swaddled by an elder of the family in wet dank blankets.
She will shortly contract pneumonia and
Be a burden to them no more.
The infant's mother sits powerless to save the life she has created,
The dowry to seal her marriage.
Crippled her own parents with debt and her with guilt.

In South Asia, a pretty toddler's mouth waters as she watches
Her brothers devour a meal.
Her body is not quite yet malnourished.
Her siblings run to school but she will be taught only to cook
And clean for her future husband's house.
She wonders what teachers smell like.

In Japan a youngster dimly remembers sunshine
From her life in Thailand
As she sews and sews hour after mind-numbing hour
The fashionable, stylish, attractive, chic shirts,
Footballs, jeans . . .
Being stitched by rutted dry, young fingers in the
Ugly, crowded filth of the rat-infested sweatshop.

In Israel, a bewildered Jewish teenager
Sits with the other 'unclean' women of the Synagogue.
She is forbidden to even read the sacred scrolls of the god
She has worshipped since birth.

In an old Catholic church a priest warns women are not like Christ.
And are not to have leadership qualities,
For 1 Corinthians tells us good Christian wives should be

Placed only in subservient roles
That demand their silence and obedience.

In the Mosque 'Quite right!' shouts the prophet Mohammed,
For we spend our wealth to maintain these women
So we are allowed authority over their lives.
Let us use Sharia Law to punish them whenever we choose!

In India an athlete looks through her one remaining eye.
She dreamed of an Olympic medal but woke up to her face
Being scorched with acid.
She was told off by her father -
She should not have refused the ugly withered old man
Who wanted to marry her.

In England a mother looks up at the glass ceiling and sighs.
She holds tight onto her daughter's hand and
Onto her hopes for her future.
She shakes her head in memory of the raised eyebrows
Of her father's golf club
When she asked to be made a member.

In Afghanistan a kind old lady clutches at her stomach in agony.
The male doctor cannot tend to her (or any woman)
By order of the Taliban Law,
But women are not allowed to be educated
So the female doctor will be a long time coming.
And we may all be dead by then.

Imogen Pierce (12)
Kirkham Grammar School

My Perfect World

I dream,
Of a perfect world,
Of a world with peace not war,
Of a world without poverty,
Or discrimination against creed and colour.

I imagine,
My perfect world,
Just as nature intended,
Peaceful and calm,
Where life runs its own sweet course.

I wish,
For my perfect world,
With no hate and no pain,
Where every man is your brother,
And every woman your sister.

I think,
Of our perfect world,
Where we are brought together,
Where children play in the beautiful sun,
There are no bad times, only good.

I hope,
That our perfect world,
Is where there is no cruelty,
Only love and friendship,
And everyone is equal.

I know,
In my perfect world,
There is no conflict,
The whole world is as one,
I dream,
Hope,
Imagine,
Think,
And wish of my perfect world.
Do you?

Liam Marrows (14)
Kirkham Grammar School

Can't You See?

A dream and a hope can be the same thing,
Although in other minds and hearts they can differ,
If you look into my eyes, can you see into my brain?
Can you see what I want in life?
Can you see what I see?

You're trapped outside, like a star suspended in the sky,
You could be a mirror image of what I want,
Just as much as the person next to you is
A mirror image of yourself,
You will just never know.

A hope or dream can be shattered in a second,
They can be melted in your mind and
Sent running through your veins,
All your nerve endings could tingle and
You just wouldn't know what to do,
But likewise, a hope or a dream can be achieved in a second,
You could be thrown towards the sky,
Lifted high above Hell, feeling the air
Gliding through your fingertips,
And yet again there would be a mirror image.

Dreams might never turn to reality
However they are always changing,
Maybe, in some minds like a tree,
At times, it's branching high and wide,
Full of confidence and hope,
But other times being slowly pushed down,
Dried out by the forces of thoughts,
So next time your dreams, hopes and even aspirations
Feel like they're falling,
Believe in yourself; remember everyone is a mirror image,
Reflecting and refracting outside of you,
And the time to grow high and wide may arrive soon.

Rosie Spedding (15)
Kirkham Grammar School

Another Victim

She innocently walks down the corridor,
Spotting them in the corner of her eye,
She holds her head high,
Feeling she might as well give it a try.

Bullying makes people self-conscious,
It's your music, hair colour, appearance,
Bullying changes people for the wrong reasons.

They barge through others coming face to face with her,
Her head now drops,
Then they stop,
So holding her head high didn't do a lot.

Bullying can make people lose friends,
Scared to go to school and learn,
Bullying can effect people's future.

So they push and shove her, making her weep,
Other kids behind a mask,
But she knows they're not to blame,
She would do the same.

Bullying when not treated can become worse,
Physical violence can be involved,
Bullying can change the appearance of someone,
So after a long day she walks home,
Feeling damaged, broken and small,
For she wonders if things will ever change,
When will she get that call,
And will she one day stand tall?

I dream one day bullying will stop,
So everyone can feel secure and happy,
With who they are,
Bullying is a killer.

Carolyn Evans (13)
Kirkham Grammar School

Is It Really Fair?

Is it fair that some have food whilst others starve?
Is it fair that some are rich whilst others are poor?
Is it fair on your grandchildren to pollute their atmosphere?

Is it right that some people die because they have no help?
Is it right to complain that you have less money
When you still have some?
Is it right to think you are better because you have lots of money?

How would you like it if you had no money for weeks on end?
How would you like to see others have lots of
                              money whilst you had none?
How would you feel if someone told you your grandparents
Polluted the atmosphere?

Would you say 'it's not my problem' if a family member
Died of a treatable disease?
Would you turn away if your best friend had no food or water?
Would you watch as your mum slowly starved to death,
Because *you* wouldn't help?

Could you watch your dad die because
The atmosphere was polluted?
Could you see your mum go to work
And earn less than £1 after 9 hours of work?
Could you listen to your kids cry themselves to sleep
Because they were so hungry?

Would you?
Could you?
Is it right?
Is it fair?

I have a dream.

Elizabeth Jenkinson (12)
Kirkham Grammar School

53

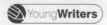

I Believe

I believe that love is a test,
I believe that we should try our best,
I believe that people should know -
Life is better taken slow,
I believe that life is fair,
I believe that we should always care,
I believe that life should be long,
I believe that we should not do wrong,
I believe that guns should be banned,
I believe that we should stand hand-in-hand,
I believe in a second chance,
I believe in love and romance,
I believe that there's always hope,
I believe that we somehow cope,
I believe in forgive and forget,
I believe in no regret,
I believe in diamond rings,
I believe in girlie things,
I believe in puppies and kittens,
I believe in furry pink mittens,
I believe in rubies and pearls,
I believe in boys and girls,
I believe in peace not war,
I believe in less not more,
I believe in giving not taking,
I believe in loving not hating,
I believe in wait and see,

But most of all, I believe in *me!*

Hannah Lewis (13)
Kirkham Grammar School

A World Without War

Imagine . . .

Gunfire, gunpowder,
Bullets, shells, missiles,
Bombs, grenades, explosions,
Boom, bang, crash,
Death.

Imagine . . .

The smell of the trench,
The rottenness of flesh,
The sound of your friend,
Wounded and crippled,
He will not survive,
Death.

Imagine . . .

Your house destroyed,
A burning wreck of nothing,
Your husband not returning,
He will never return,
Death has spoken.

Imagine . . .

Joining together,
Not fighting, not going to war,
Together, as one nation,
In harmony,
Don't let Death speak again.

Ryan Powell (13)
Kirkham Grammar School

A New God

The one reason for life,
Yet, the focus of corruption,
The different cultures blame one another,
For obscure opinion deemed fact.

Why is this idol worshipped?
No proof, no evidence, not real?
Yet, the strongest idea ever put forward
And so widely believed.

Something invisible and abstract,
Possesses people to take such trenchant action,
To sacrifice an innocent and helpless being,
When we are told to care for all living.

We are to be confused but persuaded to believe
In something so strange and inscrutable,
Imagine humankind to consider the current facts
And to see opinion as a way of finding personal amenity,
Instead of simply omitting anything that feels different.

But this will never transpire,
It would be paradise and everybody's dream,
But people will continue to fight their case,
Even if it encourages disturbing the peace.

For eternity,
This is life and it will forever be unfinished.

Lucas Christiano (16)
Kirkham Grammar School

Child Abuse

Waiting,
Not moving a muscle,
Scared stiff,
Hunched up in a ball.

Waiting,
For permission to move,
Starving from having no food,
Locked away in the dark.

Waiting,
For the hand to hit my head,
The stinging pain again and again.

Waiting,
Waiting,
Waiting,
For more and more

Abuse

There's
No
Excuse
For
Child
Abuse.

Gabrielle Thompson (12)
Kirkham Grammar School

The Perfect Harmony

Can you imagine a world full of goodness?
A world without evil and terror,
Where lives could be lived with no worry,
With peace in countries around the globe,
Living in perfect harmony.

This would be a world,
Where our neighbours are of another race or religion,
Where criminals are cleansed of badness,
Where bullets do not determine a winner and a loser.

Animals would not have to live in fear of extinction,
Those who lived in poverty would have a smile on their faces,
Victims could feel equal to oppressors,
Disease and illness would not be an issue.

Can you picture this dream world?
Trouble-free and full of happiness,
This world would be beautiful,
Sadly this is only a far-fetched dream.

Can you imagine a world full of goodness?
A world without evil and terror,
Where lives could be lived with no worry,
With peace in countries around the globe,
Living in perfect harmony.

Oliver Carpenter (13)
Kirkham Grammar School

Dreams

A dream is a hope, a wish, a desire,
It is a mixture of needs, wants or something to which one aspires,
Family, sport, home, car, career, holiday,
All determined by choices, directions, but which way?

I dream of playing hockey in a national final,
Celebrating, cheering, hugging at the final whistle,
To walk out with the first eleven,
Family, coaches gripped, it would be like Seventh Heaven.

I dream that I will be fortunate enough to affect young people,
I really want to teach, guide, inspire but
I know it will not be simple,
To work with little children is something that I would adore,
To see them grow, flourish, would motivate me even more.

A fairy-tale wedding, white satin, red roses,
Page boys, bridesmaids holding beautiful posies,
Shiny gold rings, a country home and flowers galore,
Six children, handsome husband,
What else would I need, what more?

Sandy beaches, aqua blue sea, dazzling sunshine,
A wonderful family holiday, good food, fine wine,
How expensive, how big doesn't really matter,
I just want to be content and live happily ever after!

Ally Glover (14)
Kirkham Grammar School

Helpless

I am here alone, again,
In this corner, darkness shadowing my weak and abused body,
My cheek is damp,
Damp from my tears of fear,
Is she home?
Is he home?
I hear them. Coming. Coming up the stairs,
The shouting,
Hit, punch, and scream,
My sister. Dead.
I am scared,
They're coming in here,
Should I hide?
Run away,
They stand there. Face full of anger. Murderers,
Their fist with blood,
My sister's blood,
Help me,
I'm only a child,
Helpless,
Closer and closer,
Step by step.

That's all I remember.

Georgia Gaeta-Craven (13)
Kirkham Grammar School

A Different World

In Africa there is no water,
Yet, America cannot spare a quarter,
They are grateful for a flood,
They live in houses made of mud,
We live in houses made of stone,
Yet we have the audacity to whine and moan.

In Africa, there are no crops to be found,
Yet, England cannot spare a pound,
They lose children every day,
They wish the pain would go away,
We have medics, who care and treat,
Yet our children brawl and deceit.

In Africa, they cannot use a pen,
Yet, Japan cannot spare a Yen,
They know not of games and fun,
They sizzle and perish in the blazing sun,
We have games and plenty of money,
Yet we groan if it is not sunny.

This injustice is inhumane,
People are entitled to all the same,
This should change, of that I am sure,
How would you feel if you were poor?

Lucy Newton (13)
Kirkham Grammar School

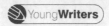

Imagine

Imagine a world where love is triumphant,
Where hate is redundant,
Where peace is everlasting.

Imagine a world where war is done,
Where famine is banished,
Where equality prevails.

Imagine a world where cruelty is finished,
Where crime is diminished,
Where race doesn't matter.

Imagine a world where religion is forgotten,
Where nations are joined,
Where poverty is conquered.

Imagine a world where we can forgive and forget,
Where money isn't respect,
Where good wins over evil.

Imagine a world where all is tranquillity,
Where hand-in-hand the people sing,
Forever and ever in harmony.

Imagine . . .

Imagine a world where you can live your dream!

Toby Davidson (12)
Kirkham Grammar School

Imagine The Hour

Imagine the morning,
When you wake up,
And the bird comes out to sing,
When racism is forgotten,
When equality arrives at your door,
When segregation has hit rock bottom,
When crime is no issue no more.

Imagine the day,
When you step outside,
And people are celebrating,
When war is finally over,
When black are at home with white,
When Man thinks it's cool to be sober,
When money isn't tight.

Imagine the hour,
When everything's done,
And people are settled at last,
When illness is at a low,
When hospitals have enough room,
When dangerous drivers go slow,
And that all of these things
Things happen soon.

Megan Kitchen (12)
Kirkham Grammar School

63

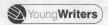

I Have A Dream

I have a dream of a world,
With no hunger,
Where all can be fed,
And famine set asunder.

I have a dream of a world,
With no war,
No violence or anger,
Just peace evermore.

I have a dream of a world,
That is just,
With race and religion,
Equality is a must.

I have a dream of a world,
Without disease,
Where all hospitals are clean,
And everyone lives life with ease.

I have a dream of a world,
That is pure,
Where all problems are gone,
And all are secure.

Robert Lavelle (12)
Kirkham Grammar School

Perfection

A world without wars, poverty or crime,
A day with more hours, so there's plenty of time,
A world without weapons, injuries or pain,
A carpet that would never ever stain,
Perfection,
A world without mockery, abuse or fighting,
A puppy that, immediately, would learn to stop biting,
A world without addiction, tobacco or drugs,
A summer with a few less annoying bugs,
Perfection,
A world without arguments would benefit us all,
Or a school without so many books to haul,
A world where it would be impossible to drown,
A computer with nothing that would ever break down,
Perfection,
A world that no one could ever enhance,
A world where everyone would have a good chance,
To do exactly what they want to in life,
And drive out all the wars and strife,
And even though a world like this would be hard to come by,
We can change ours, just as long as we try.

Jonah Winn (13)
Kirkham Grammar School

I Have A Dream . . .

I have a dream . . .
That all wars shall become extinct,
And all people of the world shall live in harmony with each other,
Despite their colour or religious belief.

I have a dream . . .
That there will be no more hunger in the world,
And children will be able to sleep at night with a full stomach,
There will be enough food to feed even the poorest countries,
And famine will become a thing of the past.

I have a dream . . .
That every child, in every country, will be able to read and write,
And will be given every opportunity to go to school or college,
They will be allowed to fulfil their aspirations.

I have a dream . . .
That the world will be a safer place to live,
Where all people feel safe in their own home,
And sickness and suffering is diminished,
Access to better healthcare will be increased for all.

Those are my dreams.

Rhys Williams (14)
Kirkham Grammar School

My Deepest Dream

Imagine
You got rid of the tears
And then there will be no fears.

Imagine
You are glad,
And you're not feeling sad.

Imagine
There are no wars
And then you will have no sores.

Imagine
Love is back,
And then all the wars we can crack.

Imagine
All the love and joy
In every father and boy.

Imagine
All the evil people that live
And all we have to do is just forgive.

Alexander James Ward (12)
Kirkham Grammar School

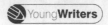

Imagine!

Imagine
Peace all around
Imagine
No wars
Imagine
I have a dream
Imagine
Poor people with houses
Imagine
One man
Imagine
That man changing lives
Imagine
Freedom and peace for all
Imagine
Countries reunited
Imagine
Hand-in-hand
Imagine
Peace . . .

Tom Middleton (13)
Kirkham Grammar School

I'm A Dreamer

Well . . . I'm a dreamer,
I dream at night . . . every night!
I dream in the day,
But not every day!

I dream about the future,
My future, the future in general,
I make the future good in my mind,
But it won't always turn out like that.

For some people the future is bleak,
For some, not even worth living,
A horrible life, full of hate and despair,
No change for a good life appearing.

We could change the future that is bad,
To a future that is good,
But only if we work together,
And dream for a good future.

I'm a dreamer,
Are you?

Sophie Breedon (13)
Kirkham Grammar School

I Have A Dream

I have a dream,
Of a place free of discrimination against race,
I have a dream,
Of a place where you can live at your own pace,
I have a dream,
Of a place without a single crime cast,
I have a dream,
Of a place full of culture and taste,
I have a dream,
Of the world being a perfect place.

Henry Hothersall (14)
Kirkham Grammar School

69

Dream

Dream, there is no war,
We are all equal,
Doesn't matter about skin colour or religion.

Dream, no worrying what other people think,
Latest phone or no phone,
Latest clothes or year-old jeans.

Dream, no crime,
People respect each other,
People respect other people's property.

Dream, the world realises the scars of global warming,
The world unites together,
The world remembers those lost in wars.

Dream, poor countries always have food and water,
No one dies of disease,
People live long, healthy lives.

Dream for the 21st century.

Bronte Edgar (14)
Kirkham Grammar School

You Need . . .

You need to understand,
That the world doesn't revolve around you.

You need to stop,
Sticking your nose in my business.

You need to see
How you're treating me.

You need to realise,
That you are hated by some.

You need to learn,
To stay out of my way.

Oliver Hulme (13)
Kirkham Grammar School

Tomorrow

Yesterday is jaded,
Seen through tinted glass,
It holds untrue memories,
Of times that did not pass.

Today sees disillusion,
Of childlike dreams from yore,
Today sees retribution,
For those things done before.

Tomorrow holds no promise,
So it cannot tell a lie,
The possibility of our dreams,
I hope will realise.

We cannot see the future,
Cannot see whether we cope,
But let us face tomorrow,
With the audacity of hope.

Arun Nantheesan (14)
Kirkham Grammar School

If You Believe In Me

Believe in me,
Have some sympathy,
Lend a hand,
Clean up your land,
Trust in one another,
Listen to your brother,
Be honest and kind,
And always use your mind,
Stick up for others and yourself,
And look after everyone's health,
Then we will all be here together,
Forever and ever and ever.

Aimee Turner (12)
Kirkham Grammar School

71

Dream

Having a dream,
Having an ambition,
Impossible it will seem,
Until you make your decision.

Fiction can be real,
Effort must be injected,
Make a personal deal,
So you are not distracted.

At times it can be dreary,
At times it can be mean,
Situations can get scary,
For some people aren't so keen.

People will benefit,
So keep your spirits high,
You have to climb the highest summit,
You will succeed if you try.

Vincent Grumme (16)
Kirkham Grammar School

Alone . . .

Alone . . . in a small room,
Separated from my brother,
No one around me,
Someone's coming . . .
Should I run?
Footsteps are coming up the stairs,
Turning towards my brother's room,
All I hear is a loud cry,
Is it my brother's
The door's flung open!
Their fists covered in blood,
My brother's blood!

Megan Butterworth (12)
Kirkham Grammar School

72

Can You Imagine?

Can you imagine,
Being all alone,
No food, no water,
Not even a home?

Can you imagine,
Looking into a mirror,
To see day by day,
You're getting thinner and thinner?

Can you imagine,
Working all day,
To have no education,
And very little pay?

Can you imagine,
That this could be you?
But if we all pulled together,
What could we do?

Lydia Dickinson (12)
Kirkham Grammar School

Many Dreams

I have a dream to change the world
I have a dream that will make a difference
I have a dream that will never end
I have a dream, a dream that inspires people.

I have a dream that the world will become one
I have a dream to stop racism
I have a dream that the world will be a happy one.

I have a dream to give everyone a chance
I have a dream that everyone will have romance
I have a dream to feed the poor
I have a dream to stop the war.

Sam Norris (13)
Kirkham Grammar School

Together We Are Strong

Together we are strong,
Joined together as one,
All sins shall be forgotten,
And God's love will reign.

Together we are strong,
We will overcome the evil,
Peace shall reign over war,
And prosperity over poverty.

Together we are strong,
The planet will be saved,
Global disasters shall end,
And hunger will be no more.

Together we are strong,
The Earth will be united,
All crime will be banished,
And God's creatures shall walk upon the Earth.

Andrew Collins (14)
Kirkham Grammar School

Dreams

I have a dream . . .
In my dream, no one is thirsty,
And everyone has food.

No one is arguing,
No one is fighting.

No one is moneyless,
No one is homeless.

The streets are safe,
And people have no need to be scared.

Anyone who is ill,
Is given help
And medicines are provided for all.

Everything is peaceful,
And that's the way it should be,
In my dream.

Sam Hall (15)
Kirkham Grammar School

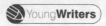

Affecting Not Just Me

My dream is one,
Which affects not just me,
But, the whole world!

Dream,
That global warming would slow down,
And the polar ice caps would stop melting.

Dream,
That polar bears could roam free all year,
With no thin ice or water to hold them back.

Dream,
Of a world with no pollution,
One in which we are not at risk.

My dream is one,
Which affects not just me,
But, the whole world!

Catherine Beesley (13)
Kirkham Grammar School

If I Could

If I could change the world,
Everybody would be equal,
If I could change the world,
Nobody would fight.

If I could change the world,
There would be no suffering,
If I could change the world,
There would be no spite.

If I could change the world,
I wouldn't,
Because things happen,
Bad and good.

Daniel Baxter Beard (13)
Kirkham Grammar School

Keep Dreaming

I have a dream that people will not pollute the Earth,
I have a dream that people will not take drugs,
I have a dream that people will not hurt or kill,
I have a dream that you will dream these same things.

I have a dream no animals will die,
I have a dream that people will not cry,
I have a dream there will be no wars,
I have a dream everyone can believe in a better future,
I have a dream that people won't hurt each other.

I have a dream no one will judge me for what I am,
I have a dream no one will complain what colour I am,
I have a dream that there will be no hunger in the world,
I have a dream people can get a proper education,
I have a dream there will be peace forever.

So just keep dreaming!

Macauley Murgatroyd (13)
Kirkham Grammar School

Life Flows By

Children and adults alike,
Run, scream, cry,
Run through deserts, ditches,
Scream for brothers, sisters, children, lovers,
Cry as they realise this is their last day,
Cry when they realise there are a million things
They'll never do, or say.

And days turn into weeks,
Weeks turn into months,
Months turn into years,
And whatever you do,
The survivors will never forget how it hurt,
And they will never heal.

Nicola Shaw (13)
Kirkham Grammar School

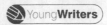

They're Just Kids

As the salty tear slowly rolls down her fragile cheek,
His foot meets her ribcage with great anger, once again,
She can barely speak, shaking vigorously, begging him to stop,
He leaves the room, slamming the door behind him, she bleeds,
She's just a kid, a child with feelings,
I don't understand why she's bleeding,
How could a father do such a crime?
One day she'll be gone, just give it time!
The little girl's body stays still, frozen,
She realises nobody notices her cry for help,
Why did Daddy do this to her? What did she do?
She's sorry she upset Daddy, she promises to never do it again,
Why do they cry?
Why do poor, innocent children die?
They have no help, they're all alone,
We can make a change!

Annabelle Mole (13)
Kirkham Grammar School

Guilty Conscience

The wistful foe lays innocently in slumber,
Unaware of the business he may be under,
The subconscious mind clouds his view,
Altering the memories he cannot undo.

Remorse enthrals his empty mind,
Rest is far from the thoughts he grinds,
The mystified mindset gracefully defies,
As he begins to grasp the pale dark lies.

Infested lies seep through the brain,
Encrusting every thought, every vein,
An unreal world slowly unveils,
Causing an envelope of twisted tales.

Katey Gabrysch (15)
Kirkham Grammar School

The Trenches

Bang!

Me and him,
All alone,
In the mist,
On the cold stone.

The blood seeped out,
Of his wound,
He screamed in pain,
He couldn't move.

His eyes closed,
The screaming stopped,
Dead silence,
And last breath.

Ben Coplestone (13)
Kirkham Grammar School

Bullying

It always happens,
Every single day,
No one knows why, but they have a hunch,
And this is what they say.

They want attention,
They want to see you unhappy,
Because they are unhappy,
They want to be the best.

It happens to hundreds of people,
In hundreds of ways as well,
Hundreds of people would be happier,
If we stop it today.

Bullying - it must be stopped today!

Matthew Donaldson (13)
Kirkham Grammar School

Dreaming

Going to bed,
My dreams ahead,
Of flying to the moon,
In my rocket shed,
I must be out of my head!

Ready to fly,
Take-off is nigh,
I feel I might cry,
I'm too scared to fly,
So high in the sky.

Above me looms,
Such a huge moon,
Like a white balloon,
Towards it I zoom,
Propelled by a spoon.

Now I'm in a car,
Driving on tar,
I'm a new rally star!
I think I'll go far,
In my super car.

The race I won,
It was so much fun,
To be on that podium,
Shouting to my mum,
And hearing the grand anthem!

Before me, it seems,
Appears a huge ice cream!
My dream sets many wild scenes,
And now on a big screen,
Comes Mr Bean!

He puts on such brilliant shows,
I don't want to go,
When it draws to a close,
My ice cream is melting slow,
And we all shout, 'No, no, no!'

So . . . I'm at the cinema,

Just been in a racing car,
Now I'm a superstar,
Doing far more than par!
Boy, these dreams take me far . . .

But this is not the end,
Now I'm negotiating a bend,
As to my bobsled I tend;
But, oh no, it needs a mend.

Crash!
The fate of my notorious sled,
As . . . I awake and bump my head!
Next to me lies old Ted,
Another day of school ahead,
Now I can't wait to get back to bed!

Lawrence Wright (15)
Longridge High School

I Have A Dream!

I have a dream to roam the world,
And see so many places,
I'll meet some people on the way,
But return to familiar faces.

I have a dream to own a mansion,
On a warm foreign island,
Nothing over the top though,
But I'd like it near the sand.

I have a dream to own a pool,
A massive private one,
I'd share it with my pretty daughter,
And even my handsome son.

I have a dream to be so rich,
But it won't happen I reckon,
So I'll live my life to the full
And enjoy every second.

Gemma Ashcroft (13)
Longridge High School

I Have A Dream

I have a dream,
We all have dreams.

I dream at night,
Sometimes in day,
Of fairy tales,
That make me giggle,
Put a smile on my face.

I have a dream,
We all have dreams.

We dream about having loads of money,
A house and fancy car,
Often for happiness,
Or something like world peace,
Or maybe just a new guitar.

I have a dream,
We all have dreams.

People have dream holidays,
In Spain or in Mauritius,
Somewhere hot,
Not usually cold,
That is, what I've been told.

I have a dream,
We all have dreams.

Some people have bigger dreams,
More meaningful perhaps,
People like Gandhi, Martin Luther King,
Dreaming for equality and peace,
Not a car, or anything.

I have a dream,
We all have dreams.

Daisy Sutcliffe (15)
Longridge High School

I Have A Dream

I have a dream one day to be,
An actress, presenter on the TV,
I'd like a cool car and a house with a spa,
They shall be the very best by far.

I have a dream one day to be,
Working with children, them and me,
To be an artist and get lots of money,
Maybe do comedy and be very funny.

I have a dream one day to be,
In a holiday cottage, near the sea,
To be a teacher, the best around,
I would like to work with music and sound.

I have a dream one day to be,
Travelling the world, the Eiffel Tower I want to see,
A graphic designer has good pay,
I would love to travel away.

I have a dream one day to be,
In a world where taxes and payments are free,
To work in a beauty salon doing people's hair,
But then I won't get to be a millionaire!

Jessica Cookson (13)
Longridge High School

I Have A Dream

I have a dream,
To be a horse rider,
To jump for gold,
And to ride to victory,
I have a dream,
To be a footballer,
To kick the ball,
In the goal,
To hear the crowd,
Shout my name,
I have a dream.

I have a dream,
To be a veterinary nurse,
To save the animals,
Of the world,
Protect them from
All the bad,
I have a dream,
To save the world,
And protect everything in it,
I have a dream.

Abby Austin
Longridge High School

I Have A Dream

I want to be a shining star,
Fancy clothes and fancy car,
Footballer's wife is the life for me,
Scoring hat-tricks 1, 2, 3,
I want to walk down the aisle,
Big white dress and a gorgeous child,
Hottest girl on the catwalk,
To London, Paris and New York,
Making money, millions a year,
Having pool parties with loads of beer,
Seeing my money roll back
Like Asda price,
Sitting there thinking, *aww, this is the life!*
I want to be the perfect mum,
To a daughter or a son,
It's not a thought, it's a destiny,
Sometimes I wonder if that life's for me,
It would be great if it all came true,
That's my dream, how about you?

Amey Leighton (13)
Longridge High School

I Have A Dream

I have a dream,
For when I grow up,
I want to be happy
And not to be snappy,
I want to have fun,
With my family and friends,
And I want that fun to never ever end,
I want to have adventures,
That are exciting and fun,
And I want to have a big house so everyone can come,
I want to be healthy,
But don't mind about wealthy,
All this I wish for me.

Alice Bateson (14)
Longridge High School

A Light Is On Its Way

A dark cloud surrounds the world today,
War and hatred rages across countries,
People suffer from hunger and disease,
Is there any hope for us in the future?

I hope for a light to break through the cloud,
A light that will rid the world of war,
Reduce poverty and disease to nothing,
The light is a saviour for everyone.

This is just my dream,
A dream that might come true,
So if I keep believing,
It might just come true.

Hannah Waters (13)
Lostock Hall Community High School

My Dream

The future world from my dreams,
Would be amazing and happy,
It would be fun but fair,
And we can make it reality.

From justice to the environment,
And prejudice to crime,
We make the real difference,
If we set it on our mind.

Whatever the colour,
Of your hair or skin,
We know it doesn't matter,
Everyone should fit in.

People don't deserve,
The abuse they get,
So what's the point?
Just give it a rest.

So people are happy,
Just do what's right,
We all know the truth,
Injustice is tight.

America's first black president,
Has just been elected into power,
All Martin Luther King's hopes and dreams,
Have reached his finest hour.

He has proved it possible,
To make a dream come true,
Now we must dream for
A better future
For me and you.

Emma Holroyd (14)
Lostock Hall Community High School

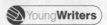

What Do I Want For The World?

What do I want for the world?
That's such a big question to ask,
No matter how many people help me,
It seems like an impossible task.

What do I want for myself?
Maybe a child or six,
But I would love to change the world,
With all my thoughts and tricks.

We are killing our homeland,
Because we can't cope without cars,
The air is full of pollution,
And now we can't see the stars.

The sun should be an orange,
But it's actually a red,
The colour is a sign of danger,
Meaning we'll soon be dead.

Our world is a terrifying place,
And it's all because of us,
Innocent people get murdered,
Or beaten on the bus.

Some people are really snobby,
They think that they're the best,
But the truth of the matter is,
They're only as good as the rest.

What do I want for the world?
That's such a big question to ask,
Maybe we should just be ourselves,
And stop hiding behind a mask.

Megan Camm
Lostock Hall Community High School

The Future Should Be Bright

I want the future to be bright,
I want people to get the treatment they need.
I want the future to be a good one,
I want nobody to be treated like a weed.

Everyone has human rights,
Basic things nations should provide,
Some people still live in poverty in this world,
I want to make sure societies remove this divide.

Nations fighting and constantly arguing,
Meaning that suffering is brought to innocent lives,
All this is slowly destroying many nations,
I want international relations to thrive.

All people are equal on this Earth,
No race or religion is better than another,
Thousands are persecuted because of this every day,
I want people to treat everyone as if they were their mother.

Ructions between neighbours, friends and relatives,
Making lives harder than they would,
This fighting slowly ripping groups apart,
I want all people to get on as they should.

People being punished for something they didn't do,
Both sides of a story need to be heard,
Many, many people are suffering for no reason,
I want all crimes to have trials, unfair punishment should not be endured.

The world is far from those highs,
But you could be the one who witnesses these changes with your eyes.

Owen Hurford (14)
Lostock Hall Community High School

Dream To Reality

Sometimes I lie awake at night
And I dream of a better life,
A place far away in my imagination,
Where only I can go,
Though I wish I could share this amazing place,
No fighting, no poverty, no grief,
I know that this world is far from our grasp,
We, as humans, are far too ignorant,
So for now I will dream,
Dream of my heroes,
Listen to my aspirations,
But through the tears and anger,
I will continue to live life to the full,
I will never give up,
If we work together we can change the world,
Strive for perfection,
No more prejudice, no more suffering,
Why are my dreams not a reality?
I wish for such simple things,
So what happens to the dream when the dreamer wakes up?

Sally-Marie Newcombe (14)
Lostock Hall Community High School

Children

My dream for the future,
Is for children's life to be fair,
Everyone should always, always care,
There is no place on this Earth for bullies,
Every child is unique,
Even though their individuality is mystique,
Some kids are funny, some are clever,
Everyone has a different personality,
Even those who are witty,
We should appreciate everybody,
Because they are just like you and me!

Holly Church
Lostock Hall Community High School

I Have A Dream

I have a dream,
I have a dream,
That dream is to be as happy,
As can be.

I have a dream,
I have a dream,
To life in a pollution-free
Place for you and me.

I have imagined,
I have imagined,
A war-free zone all over the globe.

I have imagined,
I have imagined,
A place where the word
Racism isn't a word and
We all are a family, laughing
And playing happily.

Holly Sinfield
Middleton Technology School

Just Imagine

Just imagine,
A world with peace.

Just imagine,
No more fighting.

Just imagine,
Everyone happy.

Just imagine,
No killing human beings.

Just imagine,
A place where we feel safe.

Just imagine,
People living their dreams.

Just imagine,
Everything having a place to be.

Just imagine,
A clock not being a ticking bomb.

Just imagine,
Life bad but soon to get better.

Just imagine,
One person speaking up for all.

Just imagine,
One moment of our life lasting forever.

Kirsty Chesters
Middleton Technology School

I Have A Dream . . .

A dream is a dream to be understood.

If a dream were a song, it would not be sung in a heavenly voice,
It would be sung in a child's voice, tiny, sweet and out of key.

If a dream was a beautiful woman, it would not be an angelic model, it would
be a picturesque sideways smile,
A girl gave you when you passed on by.

If your dream was a hand reaching out,
To give you the next bulging pay cheque,
Why couldn't you also dream of stretching out your hand,
Giving half of it to a little unfortunate boy on the side of the road?

If a dream was to keep a water hole full of crystal-clear water,
Would it not be obvious who would want that dream?

If anyone's dream was to paint a picture, then it is simple,
It should not be a demanding painting that takes years,
But a painting that is effortless with the brush and creates,
A heart, bound with string.

If love was a dream trying to tell you to love any living thing,
It would not be flashing pictures of nature,
With signs posted over it saying *love this and that*,
It would be you, only you,
Walking through a field and being aware of every movement,
Every flapping wing or the fluttering movement of a leaf,
That is what a dream of love is.

If any dream is dreamt and never seems to have a meaning,
Then look inside the dream,
Pick out the moving images, work them into a story,
And tell them to anyone that will listen.

A dream is a dream to be understood,
Take the minute or hour to understand them.

Aisha King (13)
Queen Elizabeth School

I Have A Dream

Is a dream real
Or is it what the mind conjures up?

I have a dream where the world will never have to stop,
To pick up the carnage of humanity,
Where the destruction of humanity is locked
In the deepest, darkest chasm.

A dream where a spark of peace,
Will burn through the hearts of humanity,
Where that spark will increase into an ever-burning
Flame of hope.

Can a dream be real,
Or is it just a lure of false hope?

I have a dream where the world will no longer dwell
On the pain inflicted by humanity
And will accept a new change in life,
A dream where people of religion and science,
Can live together without argument.

Do dreams exist
Or are they just a mist of lies blowing away?

I have a dream where people can stand up to tyranny,
And where the suffering of humans and nature itself
Are vanquished into the void of nothingness.

A dream can exist
But only if it lives in everyone's hearts.

Tom Wheatley (14)
Queen Elizabeth School

I Have A Dream!

I have a dream, a dream which has been dreamt before.
A dream where the bottomless azure seas would reflect
The crystallised sky without a flaw of pollution,
Without a hint of misuse.

I have a dream, a dream of unimaginable peace
Embedded into the minds of those evil,
Where realisation consumes the confused and leaves
Without a trace of disruption.

I have a dream beyond dreams, a thought beyond thinking,
A conclusion to cure concern of existing misery surrounding us,
To cease war,
To affirm enchanting respect between those at odds in conflict,
And to give love a second chance.

I have a dream the wind will be cleansed of its lies and scandals,
Allowing individuality to roam casually amongst the
Assembly of people,
Each with a path to follow, with a life to live.

I have a dream of complete respect,
Impossible love and freedom so unthinkable to scope,
I have a dream that Third World countries will one day sparkle
Beneath the sunlight,
With a chorus of happy voices laughing from below,
A dream that right now seems inconceivable.

Eleni Wrigglesworth (13)
Queen Elizabeth School

I Have A Dream . . .

Why can't war and unhappiness never live?
Why doesn't everyone get treated equally?
Some people say, if life is worth living,
Why don't people learn from history?

Loneliness, unhappiness and depression,
Are all a lesson to learn,
When people are sad and down,
Just give them a helping hand.

Human rights and equality should be for all,
Cruelty to animals, should be for none,
We shouldn't have racism and wars,
But most of all everyone needs someone to love.

If nobody was scared,
If nobody was lonely,
If nobody was unhappy,
Why wouldn't life be perfect?

Learn from your mistakes,
Learn from other people,
If everyone has someone to love
And someone who cares for them,
Life is worth living.

Georgia Danica Thorns (14)
Queen Elizabeth School

I Have A Dream

I have a dream, a dream for today,
Where racism and cruelty will vanish away,
For hurtful expressions, summoned upon others,
To disappear, and for us all to be brothers,
Brothers and sisters united as one,
To live on the planet to grow and blossom.

Robert Eaton (14)
Queen Elizabeth School

96

I Have A Dream

I have a dream,
That one day no one will scream,
With sheer fright,
Only pure delight,
I have a dream.

I have an ambition,
That one day everyone will have tuition,
There will be no poverty,
Only equality,
I have an ambition.

I have hope,
That one day no one will smoke,
Breathe in those fumes,
Instead of sitting on sand dunes,
I have hope.

If I had a wish,
There would be plenty of fish,
Everyone would be able to eat,
Any amount of meat,
If I had a wish.

I have a dream.

Alex Meek (13)
Queen Elizabeth School

I Have A Dream

I have a dream,
One that I want to pursue,
To change the world and make it anew.

To ban crime, conflict and war,
To destroy the poverty that haunts our streets.

Freedom, where did it go? Why are we trapped in what
Some say is a perfect world?

Talents, you have one, I have one, everyone has them,
Why not pursue these talents, share them with others?

Racism, what's the point? Black is white and white is black,
We're all the same, just treat us all as one.

Animals, what have they ever done to you,
But stand there and be your true companion?

Cancer, why is it here? Design something,
Do anything just let those innocent people live.

People on the streets, make a home for them,
All they need is care and attention,
So that one day they can try to rebuild their lives,
Don't just laugh!

Isobel Woodhouse (13)
Queen Elizabeth School

I Have A Dream

I have a dream,

My dream is paradise waiting to open,
A loving place to be,
Desire will make the world go round,
As you will soon see,

My dream is freedom for each other,
Everyone treated equally,
A heart healed will always take place,
Saving the soul deeply.

My dream will begin at the sign of sunrise,
But before we will see our memories,
A white silk throw will cover the old,
And save all the apologies.

I have a dream,

Follow my footsteps, one by one,
We will soon reach our path,
The path that will take us to our wishes,
Follow me, follow me.

Charlotte Wearden (13)
Queen Elizabeth School

I Have A Dream

I have a dream,
But you ruined it,
I had a dream of world peace,
But you ruined it,
I had a dream of equal rights,
But you ruined it,
I had a dream of happiness,
But you ruined it,
I had a dream that everyone could safely speak their mind,
But you ruined it,
I had a dream that people could live with nature,
But you ruined it,
I had a dream that people could work together,
But you ruined it,
I had a dream that everyone would be healthy,
But you ruined it,
I had a dream of life being safe,
But you ruined it.
Thanks reality!

Francis Strong (13)
Queen Elizabeth School

I Have A Dream

I have a dream for the world to be,
The very best to me personally,
Free from war, hunger, hatred, poverty,
And for free rights to all to live peacefully.

I have a dream that the world is great,
Then black and white men can mix with no hate,
For equality and world peace and fate,
For rights to education with no wait.

I have a dream that the world is fair,
That people are nice, for others they care,
That no one matches, from your feet to your hair,
And you can't judge someone by what they wear.

I have a dream that the world is keen,
To help others needing water which is clean,
Show love to animals, be nice not mean,
If I had a dream, if I had a dream.

Alex Beeson (14)
Queen Elizabeth School

I Have A Dream

I have a dream . . .
Where young children can play in the sand,
Where global warming is a thing of yesterday,
Where men don't have to fight for their land,
Where different coloured children can stand hand-in-hand,
A world of love,
A world of laughter,
A world filled with happy ever afters,
A world where no one judges,
Where everybody's equal, but no one is the same,
Where no one is hurt ever again.

Pia Grieve-Robson (13)
Queen Elizabeth School

My Own World

I have a world, which I go to high up in the sky,
This is only filled with peace and no cruelty,
I have a world, for you and I,
Just dream and you'll see.

I have a world which is hot with not a cloud in sight,
Daisies blowing in the breeze,
To be free and happy day and night,
Eating fresh fruit straight from the trees.

I have a world filled with no hatred, no screams,
No pain or sadness,
No one having to beg for life, no high-pitched, ear-splitting pleads,
No one feeling higher or less.

I have a world where I can go and dream,
Where everyone gets along,
Black people and white people can be a team,
Come on.

Jade Yorke (13)
Queen Elizabeth School

My Poem

I have a dream, a hope,
For peace to be an ambition not a war,
For honesty to be an undoubtable truth,
For jealousy to be invisible.

I have a dream, a hope,
That the world will be friends,
No crime will be committed,
No lives will come to an unnecessary end.

I have a dream, a hope,
That one day all people will be equal,
All animals will be protected,
And the world will be at peace.

I have a dream, a hope,
And one day all these will happen,
We'll just have to just wait and see.

Lucii Hardy (14)
Queen Elizabeth School

I Have A Dream

My dream is a firework ready to explode,
My dream is ready for someone to unload,
My dream is a life-changing thing,
Joy and help is all it will bring.

My dream is a loving hand to hold,
My dream will be more than a dream, once told,
My dream will abolish judgement and loneliness,
What is my dream? You have one guess.

A cure for cancer would be found,
My voice would make the sweetest sound,
Wars will stop and hearts will beat,
The love of your life everyone will meet.

Jessica Titterington (13)
Queen Elizabeth School

103

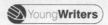

I Have A Dream

I have a dream, one dream on the list,
Where judging people should not exist,
Racism and cruelty should vanish away,
And the world will be happier from day to day,
A world where all races can stand hand-in-hand,
This won't matter and it'll be such a great land,
A beautiful place to live and a world of peace.

A world where . . .
Everyone is equal,
Everyone is unique,
People aren't treated differently for any reason,
Nobody is judged,
And everybody is loved.

I have a dream.

Mel Sharp (14)
Queen Elizabeth School

I Have A Dream

I have a dream,
To be the next James Bond,
I have a dream,
To be blonde,
I have a dream,
To save everyone,
I have a dream,
To be the caring one,
I have a dream,
To be mean,
I have a dream,
Not to be seen,
Now I have come to the end of my dream,
Although I would love to have lots of ice cream.

Ali Ahmed (11)
Queen Elizabeth's Grammar School

The Dreams I Have In A Day

As I woke up,
I had a dream,
Of a thousand robots,
Beginning to gleam.

As I got dressed,
I had a dream,
Of an alien planet,
Dusty and mean.

As I got to school,
I had a dream,
Of what it would be like,
To be a blob of cream.

As I sat at my desk,
I had a dream,
Of a couple of monkeys,
Singing along with a theme.

As I ate my lunch,
I had a dream,
Of what food would look like,
In my intestines.

As I got home,
I had a dream,
Of what it would be like,
To be in a football team.

As I went to bed,
I had a dream,
Of not being able,
To imagine and dream.

(Which was hard to imagine.)

Samuel Redfearn (12)
Queen Elizabeth's Grammar School

I Have A Dream

I have a dream,
Of raging forests,
Their knobbly roots sticking out from underneath,
I have a dream,
Of tropical birds,
Their multicoloured feathers flashing in the sunlight.

I have a dream,
Of growling tigers,
Swiftly running through the endless trees,
I have a dream,
Of roaring waterfalls,
Splashing, crashing into the shimmering pool.

I have a dream,
Of careless monkeys,
Flinging themselves from tree to tree,
I have a dream,
Of baby deer,
Fighting for survival, close by their mother's side.

I have a dream,
Of swampy lakes,
Greeny, marshy, muddy and home to many creatures,
I have a dream,
Of crocodiles and alligators,
Grinning with their razor-sharp teeth.

I have a dream.

Robert Buckley (12)
Queen Elizabeth's Grammar School

I Have A Dream . . .

I have a dream,
That one day there will be no war,
Everyone will be able to go wherever they want,
And there will be no soldiers fighting for no reason.

I have a dream,
That one day the world will be clean,
No busy cities full of cars,
Everyone will walk everywhere.

I have a dream,
That there will be no murder,
No guns used ever again,
No knives covered in human blood.

I have a dream,
That there will be no poverty,
All children will have an education,
All families will have a house.

I have a dream,
That there will be no drugs,
No stealing from deprived families,
No people taking their own lives.

I have a dream,
That I won't have a dream,
Everyone will be happy with who they are,
And everything will be perfect.

Rebecca Barnes (12)
Queen Elizabeth's Grammar School

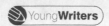

I Have A Dream

One day I dreamt I was on my skateboard,
I thought about how to speed up,
I went to chemistry one day
And there was a bottle.

And in the bottle I did find,
A bottle of nitrous oxide,
It's a flammable gas
And eureka! I had an idea!

I drew the blueprints last night,
And dreamt about my trips,
All around Blackburn,
On a rocket-powered skateboard.

With the push of a pedal,
Squeezed the bottle of nitrous oxide,
And put a lit match in the holder,
And wahoo! I flew like a bird.

I was a fast cheetah,
I shot through the shady shadows,
And with a screech I came to a halt,
Outside my own home.

Off I went to bed,
My skateboard in my head,
Then I went to sleep,
With a new dream . . . oh yeah!

Dominic Roe (12)
Queen Elizabeth's Grammar School

To John & Sally merry Christmas!

108

I Have A Dream

I had a dream that I would dive into a stream,
And the sun would shine like a light bulb,
I had a dream that the stream would be crystal clean.

I had a dream that made my eyes gleam with fright,
I had a dream that one day,
I would be a doctor,
People that were injured would be whisked into a helicopter,
To my special clinic.

I had a dream that I was in the Amazon rainforest,
It was as hot as a Bunsen burner,
I saw thousands of weird, but wonderful, creatures,
I also liked their features,
But I am not sure about the scorpion's sting,
I had a dream that I was a doctor,
I thumped the walls if my patient died.

I had a dream that I could fly high up in the clouds,
And I soared like a bird,
And dived as fast as an eagle,
But when it rained, it was truly atrocious,
Suddenly my wings began to change into arms,
I fell, I fell as fast as a bullet waiting for my end,
But it never came,
I sat up in bed,
Upright, but not dead.

Suleman Khan (11)
Queen Elizabeth's Grammar School

I Had A Dream

I had a dream one day
That I travelled far, far away,
Somewhere near the land,
But still covered in sand,
The tide came in that morning,
So I went back out at dawn.

I had a dream one day,
That I travelled far, far away,
I went to the zoo,
To see what I could do,
Then I got bitten,
By a furious kitten.

I had a dream one day,
That I travelled far, far away,
Into the desert which was really hot,
I got sunburnt a lot,
I crossed the desert that day,
So tired, down on the ground I lay.

I had a dream one day,
That I travelled far, far away,
To a land I call bed,
Where I rest my head
And to go to sleep,
To count sheep.

Tori Evans (11)
Queen Elizabeth's Grammar School

I Have A Dream

I have a dream,
I have a dream,
And it goes something like this,
Does my little dream.

I have a dream,
One day we will stand united as one,
There will be no sadness or loneliness,
For any shade or tone.

I have a dream,
One day racism will be out,
And people from all races and colours,
Will unite together and be seen out and about.

I have a dream,
One day everyone will have equal rights,
No matter what age, young or old,
Their lives will be filled with bright lights.

I have a dream,
One day it will come true this dream,
Then I will smile proudly and beam,
Look, it's come true, my dream!

I have a dream,
I have a dream.

Aneeqa Sheikh (13)
Queen Elizabeth's Grammar School

I Have A Dream

I have a dream, it makes my heart sing,
I get all excited, my ears begin to ring,
I pop and sizzle, my legs begin to shake,
It's my dream, the life that I make.

I have a dream, one day I will be,
A pharmacist, sick people I will see,
I will help them and cure them and always reassure them,
And never let them feel upset.

I have a dream that I want and will do anything to get,
I have a dream, which I will never forget.

I have a dream, that I can help people,
And bring them out of the darkness, into the light,
I will help them so they have no fear at night.

I have a dream, that I want to help them, because
If I help them they are happy and so am I.

I have a dream that I want to come true,
And I will do anything to get to.

I will chase my dream like a monkey,
Chasing after another monkey for a banana.

And this is what I want to say,
I have a dream, which I will do anything to get.

Saffa Khan (11)
Queen Elizabeth's Grammar School

Will We Ever?

Will we ever be rid,
Of that pest; world poverty?
Will we ever be able to say,
'Poverty? It's history'?

Will we ever be rid,
Of that ache that is war?
Will we ever be able to say,
'What war? War is no more!'

Will we ever be rid,
Of that sore; foreign debt?
Will we ever be able to say,
'It's all been paid, there is hope yet'?

Will we ever be rid,
Of that ulcer called crime?
Will we ever be able to say,
'Everywhere is safe, all the time'?

Will we ever?
If you try, you can,
If you don't, you can't,
That goes for everything known to Man.

Joseph Westwood (12)
Queen Elizabeth's Grammar School

Dreaming

D reaming of a better world,
R ight and wrong are seen,
E veryone is equal,
A nyone can be what they want to be,
M aybe it will happen one day,
 I hope I'm here to see it,
N othing is impossible,
G etting there is the hard bit.

Olivia Maidment (13)
Queen Elizabeth's Grammar School

I Have A Dream

I have a dream,
To play squash for my nation,
Steal their hearts,
With the skills of the best.

I have a dream,
To open a puppy farm,
To see their little faces,
Light up the owner's face.

I have a dream,
To be a geography teacher,
Teaching young people,
The fun of the subject.

I have a dream,
To be a cricket star,
Slogging it out the ground,
Or catching it behind to win the match.

I have a dream,
To be a vet,
Helping animals,
And seeing them pull through.

Nicholas Cooper (11)
Queen Elizabeth's Grammar School

I Have A Dream

Once, not so long ago, I had a dream,
I was a strawberry covered in cream!
It was very random,
Then I was in London!
I was the world's richest guy,
I was so happy I cried!
Then it went all away,
I was living in the US of A,
I was a lifeguard on the beach,
I was amazed I had to preach,
Then a woman was in big trouble,
She went under, I could only see bubbles!
I dived in the sea full of nerve and pressure,
While I was saving her, I recovered some treasure!
I was rich again, hip hip hooray!
I moved back to London before the end of the day!
It all went away again,
I had to move to Spain,
Then I woke up, back in my bed,
The dream was so crazy, it hurt my head!
Owwwwwwww!

Luke Penswick (12)
Queen Elizabeth's Grammar School

I Have A Dream

I have a dream that one day we will live in peace,
I have a dream that one day wars will not exist,
Could this be tomorrow?

I have a dream that abuse will stop,
I have a dream that drugs will not be abused,
Could this be tomorrow?

I have a dream that children don't have to grow
Up in a violent environment,
I have a dream that people will respect themselves and others,
Could this be tomorrow?

I have a dream that no one will be judged by
Their colour or beliefs
I have a dream that people won't judge each other
For what they wear,
Could this be tomorrow?

I have a dream that your dreams and my dreams will come true,
I have a dream that dreams will become realities,
Could this be tomorrow?

Millie Parker (13)
Queen Elizabeth's Grammar School

My Dream

Me:
When I am older I dream of being rich,
Hopefully having a garden the size of a football pitch,
I dream of lying on a sunny beach,
Seeing all the boats and yachts,
Maybe one day I'll have one of each,
I dream of having a sports car,
Possibly even a cocktail bar.

My dream
The world:
I have a dream,
One day I shall hope,
That every family can cope,
I can imagine the scene,
Children laughing and healthy,
I cannot remember a single impoverished scream.

Jack Kiely (12)
Queen Elizabeth's Grammar School

Dreaming - Haikus

I am dreaming of
A world without pain or hate,
Wishful dreams indeed.

Yet, maybe, change is
Just around the corner now,
We just have to try.

Climate change, disease,
World poverty, recession,
All are solvable.

A positive mind,
Ready to learn and create,
This is our answer.

Andrew Nowak (13)
Queen Elizabeth's Grammar School

I Have A Dream

I have a dream, that the world is at rest,
And everybody tries their best,
That the world is calm;
Resting in God's palm,
The wars have ended,
And poverty is mended,
Racism is no more and people are not poor,
That people treat others with care,
And hatred isn't there,
Maybe you should think twice,
Start to become nice,
Making the world a better place,
Because at the moment, it's a disgrace.

Lauren Jenkins (13)
Queen Elizabeth's Grammar School

I Have A Dream

I have a dream

H urry to the try line to score
A ll the opposition in my way
V ery risky it could be
E specially if they tackle me

A ll my teammates will support me

D riving right through the opposition
R unning as fast as I can
E veryone aiming at me
A ll eyes on me!
M y time is now!

Conor Barrett (13)
Queen Elizabeth's Grammar School

I Have A Dream

I would love to live on a farm

H orses running wild
A nimals enjoying the sweet fresh smell of the mild grass
V oices flying round in the air
E very piece of grass swaying in the direction of the wind

A pplying the horses with food and water

D reaming of what the next day will be like
R earing horses, enjoying their peaceful life
E very bit of silence following the wind
A ppetising food, freshly home-cooked
M othering horses looking after their foals.

Kate Morris (12)
Queen Elizabeth's Grammar School

I Have A Dream

I nspirational leader

H appy world
A ll war ended
V ery good life
E laborate dining

A ll food shared

D ebt-free
R adical fun
E verlasting love
A bolish poverty
M en and women equal.

Lucas Martin (12)
Queen Elizabeth's Grammar School

119

I Have A Dream Of Peace

In darkness of my eyelids and the deepness of my sleep,
I can see the perfect future, for my hopeful career.

I can see myself in my own surgery,
Trying to help those animals,
I can also see myself at weekends,
Playing table tennis with my friends.

But the best part throughout my dream,
Was the people saying,
'This is the calmest war I've ever seen.'

Now I have told you about my dream,
I can honestly say this is something to be seen.

Nathan Mann (12)
Queen Elizabeth's Grammar School

I Have A Dream

I is for mission impossible, that's what I want to do

H is for happiness
A is for ambition
V is for violence, I really wish it would stop and go away
E is for an enemy, I hope I don't get any

A is for AC Cobras, I would love to drive one

D is for disasters, they cause so much pain, I hope we help
R is for never having to pay rent
E is for extreme sports, they are really fun
A is for adventure
M is for marriage, I hope I will be happy.

Ben Souter (12)
Queen Elizabeth's Grammar School

Dream?

I dream that I will own a Ferrari and a Lamborginhi too,
I will have a big house with a patio and loo,
I will buy a jet and fly to my beach house,
I will have a business that sells computers and
Have a big wad of cash,
I will be 7 foot 2, with size 14 feet,
I will have designer shirts and shorts,
I will have a hot tub and pool and when
It is cool will warm in my pool,
I will ski down mountains and snowboard too,
I will build a rocket and fly to space.

Alex Shekleton (12)
Queen Elizabeth's Grammar School

I Have A Dream

I have a dream about the animals,
Imprisoned in a nightmare,
Cooped up in cells, living not a life,
A death.

I have a dream about life being wasted,
Like a film being thrown away,
But (you know but is a very powerful word)
A life can be used,
It can be enjoyed, looked after,
Petted with passion.

I have a dream where animals have rights,
And homes are found,
Homes which care for every animal treated badly.

That is my dream.
Thank you.

Oh and please shrink this terrifying idea of
Slavery and cruelty as soon as possible!

Barnaby Pearson (11)
St Bede's Catholic High School, Lytham St Annes

121

Global Warming

My dream is that one day global warming will be stopped,
That no more litter will be chucked on the cobbled street,
That our precious feet walk on,
That it won't be chucked in the peaceful ponds,
Where the graceful geese lay,
But is this your dream?

My dream is one day global warming will be stopped,
No more stressful, steaming gases, harming innocent people,
No more roaring gases being polluted into our own air,
But is this your dream?

My dream is one day global warming will be stopped,
That the ozone layer won't be drastically destroyed,
That it won't get anymore damaged,
But is this your dream?

My dream is one day global warming will be stopped,
That the ice caps will stop melting,
And that our independent polar bears won't become extinct,
But is this your dream?

My dream is one day global warming will be stopped,
That our beautiful nature won't be harmed,
That we will be able to see the fantastic flowers blossom,
And hear the crisp crunch of the leaves as we step on them,
But is this your dream?

My dream is one day global warming will be stopped,
We will actually be able to see our exquisite environment,
And see our natural nature,
But is this your dream?

My dream is one day global warming will be stopped,
We will be able to see the sky as clear as a crystal,
Not as black as coal, and see the bright orange sun,
We won't have to walk down the streets and be
Surrounded by coughing people,
But is this your dream?

My dream is one day global warming will be stopped,
The ozone layer will go back to its normal type,
And we will start to think about actions we do,

But is this your dream?

My dream is one day global warming will be stopped,
We will think about our invincible ice caps,
And stop our pearly white polar bears from facing extinction,
But is this your dream?

My dream is one day global warming will be stopped,
Everything will be back to normal,
And global warming will be stopped straight away,
But is this your dream?

My dream is one day global warming will be stopped,
That we will shout the freedom of this from
Every peak of magical mountains,
We will treat the wonderful world equally again,
But is this your dream?

Emma Hogarth (12)
St Bede's Catholic High School, Lytham St Annes

Poverty - Haikus

Diseased, death, dying,
Poverty needs to stop now,
Third World countries, no.

Red Nose Day has come,
We have to stop poverty,
Let's raise the money.

No showers, no loos,
It's a dugout hole for me,
No shelter, no home.

Is this water clean?
Where will I sleep tomorrow?
I'm very hungry.

Mom and Dad depressed,
Children's bellies extended,
This is poverty.

Teresa Amatiello (13)
St Bede's Catholic High School, Lytham St Annes

If I Had A Dream . . .

If I had a dream . . .
What would it be?
Money?
Fame
Or to stop a deadly disease?
Racism spreads its gruesome arms,
Drawing you into its cunning trap,
Its toxic words torture your mind,
Why does this happen?
Colour of skin should not matter,
If I had a dream . . .
What would it be?

If I had a dream . . .
What would it be?
Riches?
Clothes
Or to stop a deadly disease?
A young child,
An African child,
Has a dream too,
Hopes of a better life,
Aimlessly wander in their mind,
Their stomachs beg for food,
Food they are unable to provide,
The only way of escape,
From the vile, unfair environment they live in,
Is death,
We have so much,
They have nothing,
Is there anything we can do?
If I had a dream . . .
What would it be?

If I had a dream . . .
What would it be?
A car?
A fortune
Or to stop a deadly disease?
Pollution expands itself,

Darkening every corner,
Of our world that will not last,
Do we try,
Or are we too lazy to get up
And see the damages we have caused?
We are letting the Earth die,
As poisonous layers strangle it,
We are not being fair,
To the people in the future,
If I had a dream . . .
I know exactly what it would be!

Ellen McGrane (11)
St Bede's Catholic High School, Lytham St Annes

My Dream

I have a dream,
A dream that one day,
The people on the streets,
Will be able to buy a house.

I have a dream,
A dream to help countries,
People in the heat,
Will gain food and water.

I have a dream,
That the sick will be cured,
The poor will be wealthy,
And the lonely make friends.

My dream,
A dream upon many dreams,
That water will fill the deepest wells,
And food will fill a young child's mouth.

The people of Africa,
India, Pakistan and Asia,
Will live in peace and health.

Emily McCann (12)
St Bede's Catholic High School, Lytham St Annes

What Is The Difference?

What is the difference?
A pair of deep brown eyes
Full of sadness and grief,
Whilst other eyes
Only have time for themselves.

What is the difference?
A life full of sorrow,
Why is ours the better life?
The colour of our skin keeps us apart,
Is there such a big difference?

What is the difference?
Can't we be judged by our character
And not the colour of our skin?
We are all equal even though we
Look different on the outside.

What is the difference?
Though we come from different places,
We all are from the same world,
We should not have to stay apart,
As we can all be friends together!

What is the difference?
Just because we are different on the outside,
Does not mean we are different on the inside,
We could be more alike than you think,
We should not be kept apart.

What is the difference?
I have a dream,
There will be no more fear,
No more tears,
We will all live as one,
Whatever our religion.

What is the difference?
I have a dream,
That everyone will believe
In themselves,
They will be accepted as an equal.

What is the difference?
I have a dream,
That all people
Will hold hands as friends
And will be treated as equals in the world.

There is no difference between,
On the inside,
That should keep us so far apart,
We are all equals and should
Be treated the same.

Sarah Elliott (11)
St Bede's Catholic High School, Lytham St Annes

Satan's Little Helpers

On a day that was 9/11,
Thousands of people went to Heaven,
Satan's little helpers.

They go day by day,
Doing what their leaders say,
Satan's little helpers.

Taking millions of lives,
Turning our tides,
Satan's little helpers.

They fly their planes,
Playing their games,
Satan's little helpers.

When the buses blow up,
And people fall down,
Hearing gunshots all around,
Their AK-47s,
Send us to the heavens,
It makes us so sad,
Knowing they're so mad,
Satan's little helpers!

Matt Parkinson (12)
St Bede's Catholic High School, Lytham St Annes

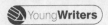

The Next Generation

I have a dream,
That one day,
Every child shall have the chance to be a child.

I have a dream,
That no child shall be harmed,
And all shall live as brothers and sisters.

I have a dream,
That every beaten child,
Will have the courage to stand up
And share their problems.

I have a dream,
That every child that is sent to the frontline,
Will go somewhere safe to be cared and cherished for.

I have a dream,
That every child shall have the hope for help,
With the NSPCC and Childline.

I have a dream,
That every child shall grow up in peace,
And not in the habitat of war.

I have a dream,
That no child shall be forced down by older people,
That they shall have the protection of a loving parent.

I have a dream,
That no child shall be forced to live on a dark street like a rat,
But shall be taken in by a carer.

I have a dream,
That every child shall stand up and be heard for their true rights,
Not sent down in flames.

I have a dream,
That this next generation of children shall be cared,
Loved, treasured, looked after, kept safe
And taught like children should.

This is my dream,
This is the next generation of children's dreams,
Can you make this dream a reality?

Laura Hall (12)
St Bede's Catholic High School, Lytham St Annes

War Is Everywhere!

I've seen it everywhere,
Innocent people thinking back to the World Wars and crying . . .
Crying for the men, the women, the children of the world
That died at the hands of those who didn't care!
I've seen it everywhere,
The different opinions of many . . .
'People shut away for doing wrong?
Or animals in a zoo waiting to die?'
Deciding whether it is right or wrong to start the next war!
I've seen it everywhere.
Many lives crushed by the news, flashing on TV screens . . .
Death, pain, terror . . . life as a horror movie,
But do you watch or join?
I've seen it everywhere . . . I've seen it all before . . .
Remember . . .
The fighters, still out there, for us!
Surely the war ended years ago,
Why start another?
I think it's time to stop it all now,
Before it gets out of hand,
Innocent people die all over the world,
Not just because of war, but of poverty as well,
I've seen it everywhere,
All the time . . . but why?

Rebecca Harrington (12)
St Bede's Catholic High School, Lytham St Annes

129

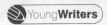
Why?

Why? Why do people treat them like trash?
Soon our relationship will rocket down to a crash,
Why do we leave them with ticks and fleas?
With cuts on their faces and bruises on their knees?
Why do we leave them to die so slowly
Thinking their lives will be easy as dough?
Why do we hurt them? Just why?

Do we think their lives are a game?
You do something wrong, so you start again,
Do you think of them unfortunate few,
That don't get love from me or you?
Do you really give a care,
When all you do is sit and stare?
Do you, do you really care?

After all these questions did you actually think,
That I will be gone in a blink?
Well I'm not!

You will see me everywhere,
I'm the protesters that really care,
I may even be living next door,
Getting angry more and more,
Until I crack, I grab the phone,
I dial the numbers, here comes the tone,
They ask what's wrong with me,
I shout, 'I'm angry!'
You may not notice, you may not care,
But soon you'll have to stare,
At the bars which trap you,
Now you know how it feels!

Do you see them in the street,
Waiting for food, waiting for meat?
Why don't you give them a home?
Give them a treat, give them a bone,
I don't really care what you do,
Just be nice to them lucky few,
Who get a loving home!

Kiera Bryan (12)
St Bede's Catholic High School, Lytham St Annes

Can I Have?

Can I have a new puppy?
Can I have a new bear?
Could I please get a new rocket,
That flies up in the air?

Can we please get some water,
Clean, clear and blue?
Can we please get some food,
And maybe some shelter too?

I can't wait till we move into our new house,
It's big and I get my own room,
My room is pink,
I have a new bed,
New toys and a TV too!

Mummy, who are those men?
Will they take our house again?
Will I go to that place,
Lose all my mates?
Will Dad get put away too?

My mum went to work today,
She dropped me at school on the way,
We had fun in PE,
I had lunch then tea,
Then I slept in my nice, warm bed.

My mum dropped us off at the park,
Then she went to sell cigarettes and cigars,
My dad left me alone,
But when I got home,
He'd slap and punch me in the head.

When the week's over,
Me and my friends play,
But the girl across the street,
Comes running out to meet
The police, while her parents run away.

Olivia Whelan (12)
St Bede's Catholic High School, Lytham St Annes

Terrible Teasing

Teasing happens too often,
Teasing happens everywhere,
Teasing happens to upset and hurt,
Teasing happens and is continuous,
Teasing is not liked.

A different hairstyle, not good enough,
New shoes, not cared for,
Latest partner, not worthwhile,
Modern glasses, not bright enough,
Teasing is not liked.

Words as sharp as broken glass,
Slicing through self-confidence,
Forcing self-consciousness,
Making mistakes self-evident,
Teasing is not liked.

Scary, poisonous thoughts,
Causing lots of unfriendliness,
Giving so much unassurance,
Scratching in uncertainty,
Teasing is not liked.

A playful phrase,
A deleterious discussion,
A nipping name,
A spiteful sneer,
Teasing is not liked.

Terrible teasing,
Taunting teasing,
Traumatic teasing,
It hurts and isn't liked,
So stop.

Katie Rhodes (13)
St Bede's Catholic High School, Lytham St Annes

Beat Bullying!

Making them feel as small as a mouse,
But inside feeling hurt and angry at themselves,
How would you feel if someone said you were ugly,
Or fat, or had a dodgy haircut?
Would you be OK with it?
People hurt other people's feelings,
Just to impress their mates,
And make them laugh,
Everyone's been a bully in their life,
As they would have said something hurtful to someone else.
Bullying not only happens to children,
It happens to adults,
Such as when they're at work,
Bullying is all because of someone being themselves,
They don't look or act like anyone else,
Bullies make weird facial expressions at you
And label you for something you're not,
As everyone is the same.
The biggest bullies of them all are the 'Populars'.
They bully others as they think they are everything,
And everyone likes them because they are
Either good-looking or have a good personality
And because they make everyone laugh,
When they say something mean and hurtful about someone else.
Most people stand up to bullies,
But the rest of them don't say a word,
And ignore them,
Because their confidence has been knocked by the bullies.
Everyone should *stand up* for what they *believe in!*
Because bullies aren't hard or clever,
So we should *beat bullying* forever!

Paige Lomax-Hurley (13)
St Bede's Catholic High School, Lytham St Annes

Well I Used To

I am black and white and fluffy all over,
I've two little babies, which are bundles of fun,
I walk through the bamboo jungle,
Well I used to!

I came across a bamboo leaf,
I felt a sigh of relief slither through my body,
At last I've found my bamboo jungle,
Well I used to!

My two little babies have something to eat,
A little bamboo and lots of milk,
But now I need a little bamboo,
Well I used to!

I came across a stream and had a little drink,
The water tasted sweet and soothing on my rough tongue,
I kept on marching through my bamboo jungle,
Well I used to!

I need to find a den to bed down for the night,
To keep my little babies warm and dry,
There is some shelter in my bamboo jungle,
Well there used to!

But now I'm so tired and want all the pain to go away,
I lie down and my cubs are sick,
They want something to eat,
Well they used to!

But now we're ill and nearly gone,
I can hear my babies' wheezy breath,
And here we lie together, side by side just drifting away,
As we share our last few moments together.

Rachel Swift (13)
St Bede's Catholic High School, Lytham St Annes

I Have Had A Dream - Haikus

I have had a dream,
Just like Martin Luther King
Justice will flow free.

Tears flow ev'ry night,
Justice shall flow by their sides,
You'll walk, walk with pride.

I have had a dream,
Just like Martin Luther King,
Justice will flow free.

The world was not made,
To be treated as it is,
It was made with love.

I have had a dream,
Just like Martin Luther King,
Justice will flow free.

There's no black or white,
Dig deeply to find your rights,
You are free to fight.

There's no black or white,
Whatever you want you fight,
There's no wrong or right!

There's no black or white,
I promise you my dream's true,
You'll be freed tonight.

I have had a dream,
Just like Martin Luther King,
Justice will flow free.

Emily Clowes (12)
St Bede's Catholic High School, Lytham St Annes

Burning Issues

(Inspired by B Dylan)

How many years can a mountain stand,
Before it is washed to the sea?
How many years can global warming,
Deprive this world of liberty?
How many years can death exist,
Before we are allowed to be free?
And how many times can a man turn his head,
And pretend that he cannot see?

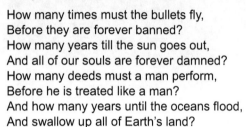

How many times must the bullets fly,
Before they are forever banned?
How many years till the sun goes out,
And all of our souls are forever damned?
How many deeds must a man perform,
Before he is treated like a man?
And how many years until the oceans flood,
And swallow up all of Earth's land?

How many times must a man look up,
Before he sees the polluted skies?
How many ears must someone have,
Before they can hear people cry?
How many times can someone drop their litter,
And leave it where it lies?
And how many deaths will it take until they know
That too many people have died?

How many of these questions will remain unanswered?
Well get out there and change some of those answers
For the better before they get worse!

Joseph Hoole (12)
St Bede's Catholic High School, Lytham St Annes

Why, Why Do People Take Lives?

Guns, knives, going through the brain,
Why do people put others in so much pain?
Bang, bang, you're dead,
'It wasn't me!' the murderer said,
Why, why, do people take lives?

You see them in a bodybag,
What are the police going to tell his dad?
A knife his dad never thought he had,
The murderer didn't get blamed, I bet he's very glad,
Why, why do people take lives?

Killing for money,
It's not very funny,
It stays on your conscious,
'My gun,' that's a load of nonsense,
Why, why do people take lives?

Beaten up, bruised with a black eye,
The murderer says, 'This is the end for you, goodbye!'
He kills him like he is some little fly,
Oh why, oh why did the poor boy have to die?
Why, why do people take lives?

Please stop with the guns, knives and the crime,
You stab them, and then you just leave them behind,
You say you have nothing to do with the weapon we find,
You will have years in prison, to be precise, 25,
Why, why do people take lives?

Ben Brown (13)
St Bede's Catholic High School, Lytham St Annes

I Have A Dream That Things Might Change

I have a dream that things might change,
That in the future, the bad things may rearrange,
I have a dream that in the future everyone will get along,
That there will be people doing right rather than doing wrong,
I have a dream that murderers won't kill, but shake your hand,
That things as simple as cigarettes will be forever banned,
I have a dream that child abuse will no longer exist,
That the abusers arrested will never be dismissed,
I have a dream that thieves will be locked away,
That they won't live to steal each day,
I have a dream that all animals will be set free,
And no longer kept in a cage with a lock and key,
I have a dream that murders happen very rare,
That if a murder does take place, the whole world will care,
I have a dream that war will eventually stop,
So that countries won't fight, be killed or shot,
I have a dream that the elderly will be able to leave their home,
That they won't be scared to walk the streets when
                                    they're on their own,
I have a dream that a boy can say what he thinks is right,
That he won't get threatened or offered a fight,
I have a dream that things might change,
That in the future, the bad things may rearrange.

Sammi Keeley (13)
St Bede's Catholic High School, Lytham St Annes

The Resurrection

Rivers of tears, will they ever stop?
Silence broken from crying men,
Sadness fills their crushed hearts,
Sad and angry memories haunt their minds,
For what they have done,
Stuttering prayers from their beaten bodies.

Stumbling, crying, walking to the tomb,
Cold, damp, darker than death,
Blood-painted cloth lying on the stony floor,
Holes in feet, could it be him?
Blue veil of happiness flying through the air,
Faces with elation,
Glow of light,
Go and spread the word.

Darkness scared away,
By the Lord,
Gentle palms from their friend,
Touch their beaten bodies,
'Is it really You?'
Frozen hearts melted with joy,
Words of forgiveness spill from His risen body,
Love overwhelmed sadness,
Nowhere to be seen,
Peace be with you!

Chloe Radford (12)
St Bede's Catholic High School, Lytham St Annes

I Hope

War, it is the old who start,
But it is the young who must fight it.

I hope,
That one day there will be no such thing as war,
That all conflict will end.

I hope,
That one day all mankind will be equal,
That everyone will love and care for each other.

I hope,
That one day all weapons will be laid down,
That weapons will never have to be used again.

I hope,
That one day everybody will be judged the same way,
That all children of different races can play together.

I hope,
That no one will be hurt because of one man's decision,
That everyone will be able to have their own choices.

I hope,
That one day everybody will be free,
That nobody will be forced to fight.

This is what I hope.

William Matthews (13)
St Bede's Catholic High School, Lytham St Annes

Crime - Haikus

We need to stop crime,
People dying in the streets,
Killers on the loose.

We need to stop crime,
Thieving from shops and houses,
People in despair.

We need to stop crime,
Houses rise with burning flames,
As hot as the sun.

We need to stop crime,
People roaming streets with guns,
Let's stop all gun crime.

We need to stop crime,
Mugging, drugs, swearing and guns,
All of this, just why?

We need to stop crime,
Violent people go away,
Let's make it happen.

All of this, just why,
All of us can help stop crime,
Come on, let's do this.

Ryan Ormerwood (12)
St Bede's Catholic High School, Lytham St Annes

Racism

Black and white at peace,
Racism should not be done,
We are all the same.

Black and white at peace,
Why do we go to war?
About racism?

What is there to hate,
About our culture or our race?
We are all the same.

We are all human beings
And inside we are the same,
Let us live in peace.

Black and white working,
Together in honesty,
Let us stay in peace.

So why did we fight,
Over nothing in the past?
We are at peace now.

Let's hope it will last,
We are brothers and sisters,
We're one together.

Oliver Mason (12)
St Bede's Catholic High School, Lytham St Annes

War

Why? Why? Why?
Why is there war
Going on anymore?

In this age of technology and peace,
Why won't people let all wars cease?
Why can't all nations be at peace?

Why did we go to Iraq?
To make sure they had no weapons,
Whilst we ourselves make countless weapons.

Why do we not allow other nations,
To make weapons like we do?
And if they don't stop making weapons,
We go in and take them.

Why do extremists blow up houses?
Because they believe God told them to,
This is ridiculous, why won't it stop?
If we dropped all our guns,
It would stop because they're not threatened.

Why? Why? Why?
Why is there war,
Going on anymore?

Silas Golightly (12)
St Bede's Catholic High School, Lytham St Annes

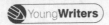

Racism

There was an old man down my street,
Who was always on his feet,
When I saw him on the Tube one day,
He dropped a bomb and was blown away.

There was an old man down my street,
Who was always on his feet,
And when I saw him in his car one day,
He dropped a bomb and was blown away.

There was an old man down my street,
Who was always on his feet,
And when I saw him on his bike one day,
He shot a rocket launcher at some normal people one day,
Killed them all and cycled away.

There was an old man down my street,
Who was always on his feet,
And when I saw him on a plane one day,
Let out some poisonous gas,
And gassed everyone away.

This man was a dope,
He shouldn't have done
What he had done!

Callum Best (11)
St Bede's Catholic High School, Lytham St Annes

Racism: I Have A Dream

I have a dream,
That black and white
Are the same because this, this is no game,
I have a dream.

I have a dream,
That we'll be like peas in a pod,
No difference at all,
And only get judged by what we do,
I have a dream.

I have a dream,
That we can just get along,
Because what have they done?
Are you doing this for fun?
I have a dream.

I have a dream,
That we can sing a song for once,
For once I wish that we could be like a keyboard,
Ebony and ivory sitting together,
Could we do something so simple?
I have a dream.

Ellie Ghee (12)
St Bede's Catholic High School, Lytham St Annes

Poverty!

I have a vision.

A vision where poverty is over and all the people in Africa
And Iraq will have a secure roof to live under,
A vision where the children will be properly educated
And provided with school equipment,
A vision where people in poverty will be given clean water
And plenty of food to eat.

I have a vision.

A vision that all the people of all the countries
In the world come together and make a small donation
To people in poverty so they can afford home essentials,
A vision where everyone is treated the same
And not differently because they have less money and no home,
A vision where people of all ages get the treatment
And the care they need when they are sick.

I have a vision that we all join in and make a donation
And poverty will be stopped.

This is my vision.

Kelly Birnie (12)
St Bede's Catholic High School, Lytham St Annes

Paedophiles

Why do they watch all the time?
They are committing a serious crime!
Evil is what they are made of,
They are as dark as Death itself,
Stalking from corners and walking at night,
Living out their disgusting lives,
They are paedophiles.

Trafficking, selling, and sinning,
The cursed ones they are,
Lives meaning nothing,
Pouncing out from the dark,
They don't listen, they don't care!
Beware! They're everywhere!
And they are paedophiles.

So when you walk in the dark,
Don't talk to strangers,
Don't make the worst mistake,
The life-threatening one,
Of trusting paedophiles.

Giuseppe Dal Prá (13)
St Bede's Catholic High School, Lytham St Annes

I Have A Dream For The Future

The future could look so much brighter,
Without all those criminals, guns, knives and fighters,
Why does the world have to be so wrong?
Turning children into killers instead of them listening to songs,
Gangs of hoodies hanging around,
When all they really want is to be stood on solid ground,
Child abusers roaming the streets,
Let's help crack down so we can all sit comfortably in our seats,
Racism seems to be taking over in the main,
So please let's teach these people we're all the same,
It seems so wrong when I'm at home,
Thinking about all the people living in poverty on their own,
On the news, we just seem to hear the doom and gloom,
Credit Crunch is becoming a main part of our lives soon,
All these problems aren't helping us out,
In fact, all they're doing is causing hassle and problems to sort out,
So let's put a stop to all these nightmares,
And give people of the future a better, safer world to share.

Bethany Sorah (14)
St Bede's Catholic High School, Lytham St Annes

I Have A Dream

R aces are equal
A ll men and women should be treated the same
C ultures split us up
I ndians, Chinese and Pakistanis should be treated the same
S eeds of hope unite us
M ountains of despair separate us

W ill they ever stop?
A fghanistan has one
R acism starts a lot of them
S egregation causes the fighting.

Benjamin Huddleston (13)
St Bede's Catholic High School, Lytham St Annes

148

Free Verse Poem

I have a dream
That in the future
There will be no wars

I have a dream that everyone can be free
I have a dream
That everyone can live a happy life

I have a dream that there will be a bright tomorrow
I have a dream that everyone can wake up for a bright day

I have a dream for world peace
I have a dream that everyone can go outside and feel alive

I have a dream that everyone can enjoy every day
I have a dream

I have a dream that the world can be lit up
I have a dream that they can feel safe

I have a dream.

Mark Drinnan (12)
St Bede's Catholic High School, Lytham St Annes

I Have A Dream

	I	believe in justice
People	H	aving enough food
	A	world in which everyone is kind
An en	V	ironment that will not be destroyed
	E	quality
	A	fair, equal society
Hopefully my	D	ream will one day become reality
	R	acism will go
People become	E	nvironmentally-friendly
	A	world in which no one kills
All	M	en and women are equal.

Curtis Clough (13)
St Bede's Catholic High School, Lytham St Annes

I Have A Dream

One day this world,
Will be a different place,
With peace and love,
Throughout the human race.

War and crime rates,
Are going to drop,
And global warming,
Will completely stop.

No more racism,
Poverty, famine or hurt,
Through our mistakes,
The lessons are learnt.

I have a dream,
That one day may come true,
But to make this change,
We must start anew.

Hannah Smith (14)
St Bede's Catholic High School, Lytham St Annes

I Have A Dream

I have a dream,
That one day there will be no more racism,
No more headlines about people being shot,
Because of the colour of their skin.

I have a dream,
That people will be able to become one nation together,
People will be free to be who they want to be.

I have a dream,
That everyone will be able to join hands
Like brothers and sisters at last.

I have a dream.

Esther Goode
St Bede's Catholic High School, Lytham St Annes

I Have A Dream

I have a dream that one day we will all be equal,
The rich shall share their money with the poor,
To make money change lives for sure,
Everyone shall have access to fresh food and water,
Treat everyone with respect as if they were your daughter,
We will help and support the poorer countries,
Making sure we see to everybody's needs,
No longer shall people suffer in silence,
There shall be no mention of violence,
As always we must not forget,
To give everyone respect,
As God created us all in the same way,
And asked us to enjoy our life day by day.

I have a dream that we will all be together as one big family,
And live in peace and harmony.

Katie Lambert (14)
St Bede's Catholic High School, Lytham St Annes

An Animal's Plight

Animal abuse is as dark as night,
It will never be a happy sight.

It's heart-rending to see an animal that is hurt,
Abused, in pain and treated like dirt.

No animal should have to suffer from hunger and the cold,
This animal is not even old.

He abandoned the animal, it was now lost and alone,
How will it ever find happiness and a loving home?

But, miracles do happen all the time,
There are good people in this rhyme,

This desperate dog was found!
And now has love all around.

Darcey Myers (12)
St Bede's Catholic High School, Lytham St Annes

151

I Have A Dream

I live in hope that one day terrorism in the world will end,
And that terrorists will realise what it is they're doing,
That some kind person will have a hand to lend,
To stop the problem of terrorism and loss of innocent lives,
Make the terrorists stop these terrible things,
So people can board planes with no fear of death,
9/11 was an eye-opener to the world,
Showing everyone these people have no mercy,
If these crazy people could see their actions are helping no one,
Then maybe, just maybe, they would stop,
Stop terrorism now, it is very bad,
We are fighting in a war that we never should have had,
Guns, violence, knives and bombs,
No one knows who and where the bomber is from.

Joel Courtney-Whiteside (14)
St Bede's Catholic High School, Lytham St Annes

I Have A Vision . . .

To see all people together,
I have a vision of a dark yesterday and a bright tomorrow,
People will live together as one instead of two,
To see children play and hold hands in perfect harmony,
No rules on where black people stand,
No rules on where *anyone* stands!

I have a vision to see white people
In the same room as black people,
With no issues of each other!
I have a vision to see the world happy and peaceful,
Instead of rich and in slavery!
Everyone working as one -
Everyone classed as one!

Sophie Gwilt (12)
St Bede's Catholic High School, Lytham St Annes

Animal Cruelty

Whimpering echoes through houses,
Starving dogs left on floors, dying.

Shivering rattles pavements,
Freezing rabbits left in hutches, dying.

Scratching sounds fill porches,
Forgotten cats stood on doorsteps, dying.

Silence fills cellars,
Suffocating illegal snakes left in over-heated tanks,
Dying.

The sound of dying animals fills the Earth,
Animal cruelty, it's everywhere!

Ellen Bradley (11)
St Bede's Catholic High School, Lytham St Annes

Bullying

Don't bully, be nice,
Before you do it, think twice,
In the house, in school,
Yeah, that's right, bullying's so not cool,
Bullies are cowards, pathetic and sad,
They are not big, not hard, not bad,
Just cos they've got the brand new gear,
Don't give you the right to make 'em fear,
Just cos they're different, not like you,
They're individual and you should be too,
Be a shepherd, not a sheep,
Don't make the victims cry and weep!

Amy Fielding (14) & Leah
The Derby High School

153

I Have A Wish!

If I had one wish we'd be treated the same,
No matter what was our name,
If I had one wish we'd all be friends,
The love would never end,
This is what I wish . . .
All those racist faces would go,
Leaving not even the one,
This is my wish . . .
Who says we have to be one colour?
I say it's better if we are different to each other,
This is my wish,
So what's wrong with this?
All of you who hate, stop and don't diss,
This is my wish,
No one should be sad,
So think, all of you who are bad,
This is my wish . . .
Let's stop any of those who fight,
Because these people are just not right!
This is my wish . . .
Why can't we all hold hands and be a happy nation,
All together we can kick away the devastation,
This is my wish!

Zahra Hafeez (13)
The Derby High School

War

War in Afghanistan,
Locals were doomed,
Afghans would take over,
That's what people assumed.

Help from the US and Britain,
Even Afghan police,
All the people wanted,
Was for there to be peace.

Soldiers fighting,
Either being injured or dead,
They want to come home,
They miss their bed.

Families and friends,
Mourning in grief,
All they want to do,
Is turn over a new leaf.

US and Britain,
Are slowly winning the war,
But what everyone wants to know,
How long can this go on for?

Daniel Smethurst (13)
The Derby High School

Young Writers Information

We hope you have enjoyed reading this
book - and that you will continue to enjoy it
in the coming years.

If you like reading and writing poetry drop
us a line, or give us a call, and we'll send
you a free information pack.

Alternatively if you would like to order further
copies of this book or any of our other titles,
then please give us a call or log onto our
website at www.youngwriters.co.uk

Young Writers Information
Remus House
Coltsfoot Drive
Peterborough
PE2 9JX
(01733) 890066